{ THIS BOOK BELONGS TO }

....

Shannah Kennedy is a leading Australian business and life coach whose expertise enables clients to gain control of their lives and achieve their visions and goals. An Advanced Certified Coach and NLP practitioner, Shannah works individually and in groups with a diverse range of executives, entrepreneurs and sporting leaders, including Olympians and CEOs. As a coach, she uses her skills, energy, ambition, drive and spirit to motivate and inspire others to turn their dreams for their lives, careers and business into reality.

shannahkennedy.com

This book is dedicated to my husband, Michael, who encourages me to stretch myself, and to my children, Jack and Mia, who help me keep life simple and clear.

This book is also dedicated to you, the reader, and to my wonderful clients and social media followers, whose praise and gratitude gave me the courage to write it. Fill it with your thoughts so it reminds you of who you really are and where you're going in life.

The Life Plan.

Simple Strategies for a Meaningful Life

Shannah Kennedy

Photography by Sharyn Cairns

LANTERN

an imprint of
PENGUIN BOOKS

Your thoughts create your world.

Health is my Wealth

Blessed are those who see beautiful things in places others see nothing

A NOTE
FROM SHANNAH
—

This book will show you my simple tools to make life bigger, better, more meaningful and whole, and healthier, both personally and professionally. My approach is for optimal living in all areas of my life; the business of *me* is my first and foremost job – everything else comes after that.

Throughout my years of coaching, I have found that most of my clients share one commonality – they don't need motivation. They're very successful people and they know what they need to do to reach their goals. What they actually require is for things to be simplified, so they can get back to the foundations of who they are, dig themselves out of the clutter to find clarity and purpose in their daily routines, and live a full life without self-destructing in the process. In this book, I share the tools I've developed with my clients over the years to help them do that.

My life has been a truly big journey. I think I wanted that from the day I was born. When I saw the movie *Wall Street* in 1987, I was seventeen years old and trying to decide what do with my life. All of that power, wealth and success was hugely appealing to my adolescent self, so I committed to getting a job at a high-profile stockbroking firm – and pulled it off. But there was increasing pressure to gain a degree and I hated studying, so after a few years I chose more life experience and began looking for my next chapter.

Aged twenty-one, I set off to explore the world. I backpacked around Europe, the Middle East and parts of Africa, working my way through kitchens and bars. I slept under the stars high in the Atlas Mountains of Morocco, dozed on a small wooden boat on the river Nile, swam in the Dead Sea and waitressed in the ski resort of Mürren, Switzerland, home › of the James Bond 007 revolving restaurant. I hitchhiked through Spain, sleeping on many rooftops and staying everywhere from basic rooms to the odd grand castle. It was the most wonderful adventure.

After two years I came home and went back to the stockbroking firm, but I didn't feel challenged. Trying to be true to myself, I decided to swap numbers and stress for something completely different, and took up an assistant role in a golf management company. Soon I was negotiating contracts, managing professional golfers, travelling on tours, organising corporate golf days and learning everything there was to know about running a business from the ground up. It was a time of major growth.

Then, as often happens when you least expect it, life threw me a curve ball and I was asked to join a high-profile sports eyewear company as their sponsorship and PR manager. Overnight I went from managing a dozen golfers to working with more than 100 world-class athletes in Australia and internationally. By most people's definition of success, I was living the dream. It was exhilarating, satisfying and demanding all at once. It was also incredibly intense.

As a high achiever I was used to overloading my life, so when the stress and exhaustion mounted I brushed these warning signs aside as the price to be paid for the kind of success I craved. I believed I was strong and nothing was going to hold me back from having everything I wanted. I was both unwilling and unable to slow down, and eventually my body delivered a devastating reminder of its need to be cared for, abruptly giving way to chronic fatigue syndrome (CFS).

It was debilitating. Virtually bed-ridden for twelve months, I lost everything that mattered to me – my sense of self, my network, my ability to do the simplest things. My body just wouldn't respond. Sinking towards depression, I felt overwhelmed with shame and failure, replaying why things had gone so wrong over and over in my mind.

It took me a long, slow three years to fully recover, but with help from a life coach I eventually regained my energy, clarity and motivation to move on. It took several more years before I realised what a blessing my illness really was – a gift that allowed me to see life's grand picture.

I have also (unforgettably) witnessed many elite athletes self-destruct once their sporting careers were over. This, as well as my own experience ›

with burnout, inspired me to get over my distaste for study and embrace extensive training to become an Advanced Certified Coach. Who would have known I could be a committed student? I could see an opportunity to coach sportspeople to become whole people rather than has-beens, with the purpose and vision to create the life they want, both during and after their short athletic careers.

During this productive time, I loved taking myself away to health retreats to recuperate and recharge. I recognised that I also needed to find a way to integrate these stress-busting, restorative strategies into my everyday life. It's no good if you can only find that clarity when you're away from your ordinary life. So I have tried and tested strategies to get that balance – to find depth and calm in my work, joy and contentment in my family, and vitality and vibrancy in my life. To build a rock-solid foundation based on my purpose; a valuable, personal definition of success to guide my choices and behaviours as I go through life. To do whatever I can and live without regrets.

Over a decade on, it's my passion for managing time so it works for us, rather than against us, that means my services are in constant demand. We all want a good life, but this has become increasingly challenging for many of us as we're mentally ambushed at work, over-connected digitally and yet under-connected in our most important relationships.

Working within large corporations coaching senior executives, sales teams, individual business owners and contractors, I always focus on the foundations. By going back to the basics, we can regain control and therefore make clear, informed decisions and also build supportive habits to create lives we love living.

Over the years, the structures that are outlined in this book have guided strategies for employee engagement, inspired valuable team-building activities and provided powerful tools to connect leaders with their teams. They have proven to be effective not only for managers, leaders, entrepreneurs and business owners, but anyone who wants to set and achieve clear goals, create success on their own terms, foster meaningful relationships and live each day to the fullest, with a sense of depth, strength and sustainability. They have empowered every client I have coached, whether they are a stay-at-home mum, small business operator, multi-millionaire or elite athlete. ›

With all this going on, my life was soon humming along: happy marriage, two healthy children at school, the house renovated and my business booming. My first book *Simplify, Structure, Succeed* was in its third print run, having proven itself to be a tool my clients loved. The seeds I'd planted along my journey were all coming into bloom. So I decided it was the perfect time to shut up shop – at least for a few months.

It was time to press the 'pause' button on life, to get the courage to walk away from all that was comfortable, to grow, to connect with myself and my family unit at a whole different level, all while facing the possibility that my business might be gone by the time we came home. Our mini-sabbatical of five months away was an investment in our life strategy, a serious mental and physical deposit into our lives to avoid burnout and mental fatigue. I share this story with you in the book, and I have committed to taking mini-breaks on an ongoing basis, rather than waiting to retire to live my life's adventures.

This book is for your life strategy, to help you get back to your foundations, to understand what life looks like at your best and to prepare your future intentions so the road ahead is clear, inspiring and full of success.

This book is about integrating the things that most people only discover when they hit rock bottom into your everyday life. It is about taking things one day at a time so you can start forming habits that become a way of life and giving each moment the potential to take you closer to the way you want to live. It is your personal life coach. It is a place to plan, visualise, reflect and prioritise. It is a place to start, simplify and succeed. A place for the fundamental work to be done. It is a practical guide to effective life planning.

Yours in intentional, optimal living,
Shannah

P.S. Remember, it is not just about what you *get* by accomplishing your goals and achieving success, but also about *who you become* through the process.

Get out of the
passenger seat
and into the
driver's seat.
Driving is
a blast!

START

—

Knowing yourself is the beginning of all wisdom.

—

Aristotle

START

—

Who are you? This is one of the first questions I ask every new client and the incredible thing is, most cannot answer it. Many of us rely on our work to define our sense of ourselves, but I ask clients to think about who they are outside of that.

You might be a CEO, an entrepreneur, an executive, an office worker or a creative artist, but while this is what you do, at the end of the day it's not who you are. Parent, employee, boss, landlord, partner, husband, wife, investor, client, friend, sister, uncle, business owner, soccer coach, coffee aficionado . . . These are all examples of the many different hats we wear in our everyday lives. But these are roles we play, rather than who we are at our very core.

Finding out exactly who you are away from all these tasks and roles is liberating and offers insight into whether you're on track, or perhaps way off it. The question is actually less, 'Who am I?', and more, 'Who am I without my job, partner, career, home, car, hobbies, kids and family?'

At your current stage of life you have had a tapestry of valuable life experiences. Some will have been great, some good, others okay and no doubt some will have been bad, but each one has shaped who you are today. Together they provide you with all the information you need to tell you who you are and who you want to be.

What's the story of your life so far?

Take a quick look at how you got to this point in your life, without getting caught up in the emotion of past experiences. Simply write down the experiences that have shaped you the most as a person.

YOUR LIFE LINE

0

10

15

20

25

30

35

40

45

50

55

60

65

70

So really,
who are you?

Every action we take is preceded by a question, whether we know it or not. It could be as simple as: 'Do I want to do this?' Yet often we're completely unaware of the questions we ask ourselves or how they shape our lives.

Learning to tune in to these questions is one of the most powerful ways to start finding the insight, inspiration and authenticity to live the life you really want. It cuts through the fog and overload in your mind to give clarity and simplify the picture of who you are and what you are trying to achieve. It also builds your self-esteem and confidence as you discover that many of the answers you are seeking lie within.

These questions will help you get started on the process of clearly defining who you are. Take time to consider each question fully and honestly, as they provide the framework that you will later use to establish your values.

WHO/WHAT IS MOST IMPORTANT TO YOU?

....

WHO/WHAT ARE YOU INSPIRED BY AND WHY?

....

WHAT MAKES YOU SMILE OR BRINGS YOU SHEER DELIGHT?

....

WHEN HAVE FELT YOU WERE AT YOUR BEST, MOST PASSIONATE
AND ALIVE?

....

WHAT ARE YOUR NATURAL GIFTS AND ABILITIES?

WHAT DO YOU LIKE ABOUT YOURSELF?

WHAT MISTAKES HAVE YOU LEARNT FROM?

WHAT HARDSHIPS HAVE YOU OVERCOME?

WHAT ARE YOU AFRAID OF?

HOW DO YOU WANT TO BE REMEMBERED BY YOUR FRIENDS
AND FAMILY?

WHAT DO YOU REALLY WANT FOR YOUR FUTURE?

WHO DO YOU NEED PERMISSION FROM TO START
TAKING RESPONSIBILITY?

WHAT ARE YOU CHOOSING TO DO?

WHAT AREAS OF YOUR LIFE DO YOU MOST WANT TO MOVE FORWARD IN?

* *Make a pact with yourself to be YOU Incorporated, and no-one else.
Be proud of who you are.*

WHO ARE YOU WHEN YOU'RE AT YOUR BEST?

Are you clear about what's true, good and possible when it comes to who you are? Unfortunately, many of us tend to dwell on our failures. Stories of our worst moments tend to linger far too long, while stories of our best moments fade all too fast. Most of us are so busy churning along on the treadmill of everyday life that we tend to gloss over our achievements.

Take a moment to think back on the last few times you felt you were really engaged, energised and enjoying your life.

WHAT WAS HAPPENING?

....

WHAT WERE YOU DOING AT THE TIME?

....

WHO WERE YOU WITH?

....

HOW DID IT FEEL TO BE THIS PERSON?

....

WHY ARE YOU PROUD OF THIS MOMENT?

....

These might be big or small moments. They might be at work, at home or at play. They might be long or short moments. Every moment at your best is worth remembering, as it helps you find ways to spend more time being who you're capable of being.

When you understand and own your best moments you improve your sense of confidence and your ability to create more moments like these. Savouring your successes allows you to build your confidence, fuel your optimism and motivate yourself to keep moving on.

Often people attempt to
live their lives backwards;
they try to have more
things, or more money,
in order to do more of
what they want so they will
be happier. The way it actually
works is the reverse.
You must first BE
who you really are, then
DO what you need to do,
in order to HAVE
what you want.

—

Margaret Young

What is
your purpose in life?

Of all the questions I ask myself, by far the most powerful is the one that I start with each morning: What is the purpose of today?

My purpose in life is to live it fully and to make the most of what I have been given. But when I break it down daily by asking 'What is my purpose today?', I make real leaps forward in my level of happiness and sense of achievement.

To have purpose is to feel connected to something bigger than ourselves – be it a religion, community, sporting club, a cause or just a reason to get out of bed each morning. It gives us something to aim for and helps to clarify our intentions. It also inspires us and makes our hearts and bellies warm with excitement.

For some of us, purpose is grounded in popularity, power and money. For others, the focus is growth and contribution. What matters most is that we pursue our purpose for the right reasons – because it's something we deeply believe in, rather than something someone else is steering us towards.

QUESTIONS TO DISCOVER YOUR PURPOSE

- ➤ How do you want to be remembered and what can you do to be that person?
- ➤ What messages do you want to give your children?
- ➤ What difference will others say you made in this world?
- ➤ What do you want to achieve in your life?
- ➤ How do you want to feel as you move through each day?
- ➤ When you are your best possible self, who might you be?
- ➤ How can you serve others?

* *Be grateful along the way.*

What do you value?
The key to you

Defining your values is the next major step to unlocking your success. Values are those things that really matter to you – the ideas and beliefs you deem to be the most important in your life.

A range of factors, including your background, upbringing, spiritual beliefs, life philosophy and events that you've experienced or witnessed will all shape the values you hold. Values have a major influence on your behaviour and serve as broad guidelines to make authentic choices that leave you feeling more content, happy and satisfied as life unfolds. When your actions aren't in alignment with your values, you find yourself without a sense of achievement or feeling out of control.

The best day of your life is the day on which you decide to own your set of values and live by them. Do you know what your values are? Are you living your life accordingly?

MY TOP THREE VALUES

My top three values are health (physical and mental), the happiness of my family, and having a sense of achievement daily. Understanding my values brings absolute clarity to every decision I make.

The characteristics I want to project are calm, confidence and fun. I aim to keep my body strong, to travel with purpose, to keep my marriage fun and inspirational, and my business constantly evolving.

In the past, my sense of achievement was gained from doing more – being more efficient and more productive, and succeeding in sport and business. However, it's evolved to include the more nourishing elements of space, valuing the downtime just as much as the busy times, and realising that even doing simple chores is an achievement.

---

* *Make a deliberate and conscious effort to identify, and live according to, your values.*

DEFINING YOUR VALUES

1 | **SELECT**
Identify your top ten values, choosing from the box to the right.
Don't spend too much time agonising over your decisions:
go with your gut instinct.

2 | **PRIORITISE**
Prioritise each value from one to ten. Focus on your top five
and briefly define what each one means to you.

3 | **CONTEMPLATE**
Read each value slowly, letting the meaning of each word sink
in so that you fully understand what each one means to you.

4 | **DEFINE**
Select your top three values and write them down. Commit
them to memory, as they will now act as your decision-
making blueprint. You also need to define the single value
that is most important to you.

5 | **COMMIT**
Work out what you need to add or remove from your life and
what you need to change to reflect these values.

---

* *I program my phone to greet me with my values each morning. It is an instant
reminder that all my decisions need to be in alignment with my values. They
then become confident decisions, and I become a confident decision-maker.*

FAMILY HAPPINESS Quality time, bonding	**SELF-RESPECT** Sense of personal identity, pride	**GENEROSITY** Helping others, improving society
COMPETITIVENESS Winning, taking risks	**RECOGNITION** Acknowledgement, status	**WISDOM** Discovering and understanding knowledge
FRIENDSHIP Close relationships with others	**ADVANCEMENT** Promotions	**SPIRITUALITY** Strong religious and/or spiritual beliefs
AFFECTION Love, caring	**HEALTH** Mental, physical	**LOYALTY** Devotion, trustworthiness
COOPERATION Working well with others, teamwork	**RESPONSIBILITY** Being accountable for results	**CULTURE** Traditions, customs, beliefs
ADVENTURE New challenges	**FAME** Public recognition	**INNER HARMONY** Being at peace
ACHIEVEMENT A sense of accomplishment	**INVOLVEMENT** Belonging, being involved with others	**ORDER** Stability, conformity, tranquillity
WEALTH Getting rich, making money	**ECONOMIC SECURITY** Strong and consistent income streams	**CREATIVITY** Being imaginative, innovative
ENERGY Vitality, vim, vigour	**PLEASURE** Fun, laughter, a leisurely lifestyle	**INTEGRITY** Honesty, sincerity, standing up for oneself
FREEDOM Independence, autonomy	**POWER** Control, authority or influence over others	**PERSONAL DEVELOPMENT** Use of personal potential

What lessons
have you learnt?

What have been your greatest life lessons so far? The purpose of asking this question is not to become lost in introspection. Rather, it is to prevent you making the same mistakes so that you can grow, evolve and continue to learn.

Your greatest lessons help to shape you into the person you are, and although they can be painful, many lessons ultimately make life more enjoyable and rewarding.

For instance, after suffering from chronic fatigue syndrome that was brought on by trying to achieve too much, I learnt that whenever I say 'yes' to anything – a job, an opportunity, a favour or an invitation – there is a cost involved. So I need to be aware of that cost, whether it is to my health, family time or finances, before making any decisions.

Are your problems recurring ones from the past? They become habits and a pattern when we don't stop to acknowledge them, address them and learn from them. Creating a strategy so they don't happen again is critical. Why does the same thing keep happening to you? Do you really care enough to do something about it once and for all? How can you now make a difference?

Emotionally intelligent leaders strive to learn from mistakes, because they know how valuable they are for growth – personal and professional – and your ability to move forward.

---

*   *Your greatest lessons help to shape you into the person you are.*

SOME POPULAR LESSONS

1   When in doubt, just take the next small step.

2   Don't take yourself so seriously. No-one else does.

3   Pay off your credit cards each month.

4   You don't have to win every argument. Agree to disagree.

5   Cry with someone. It's more healing than crying alone.

6   Make peace with your past so it won't screw up the present and the future.

7   Don't compare your life with the lives of others. You have no idea what their journey is about.

8   A writer writes. If you want to be a writer, write.

9   It is never too late to have a happy childhood. But the second one is up to you.

10   Burn the candles, use the nice sheets. Don't save them for a special occasion. Today is special.

11   Over-prepare and then go with the flow.

12   Be eccentric now. Don't wait for old age to dye your hair pink and wear purple.

13   Frame every so-called disaster with these words: 'Will this matter in five years' time?'

14   However good or bad a situation is, it will change.

15   Get outside every day. Miracles are waiting everywhere.

16   Take a deep breath. It calms the mind.

17   If you don't ask, you don't get.

What are your golden moments?

What are the memories you treasure? These are tiny snapshots for you to take daily; they're to be cherished and archived in your mind forever. There is gold around you all the time if you choose to look for it, engage and be present. This is what gives depth to our lives.

- Noticing the first blossom on a tree.
- Walking out of an interview or meeting, and knowing you've nailed it.
- Gazing at the stars at night.
- Feeling the sand between your toes at the beach.
- The shape of water as it drips down a window.
- Catching a glimpse of your partner daydreaming.
- Seeing a perfectly formed daisy.
- Hearing your child give a real belly laugh.
- Stopping to listen to a busker playing beautiful music.
- Being promoted or offered a new job.
- The smell of really good coffee.
- Passing a test or exam with flying colours.

This simple act of mindfulness, of tuning in and being truly present to the small wonders unfolding all around you, while calmly acknowledging and accepting your thoughts, feelings and bodily sensations, is an oasis you can tap into anywhere, at any time.

Look for, and savour, the golden moments happening all around you, each and every day. Collect these treasured moments and use them to guide your vision of success.

＊ *To be mindful means to dwell deeply in the present moment.*

What is your definition of success?

Before you start striving for success, it's important to identify exactly what it means to you. And, just as importantly, how you will measure the way success is unfolding in your life.

There's no right or wrong way to define success – it is simply what matters most to you. It's crucial to identify your own criteria, because achieving success (and feeling successful) is where you want to invest your energy and effort on a daily basis. I feel that success is your complete body of work in life; it's you as a whole package.

- ➤ How does success feel to you?
- ➤ How would you define success in one sentence?
- ➤ How will you measure it daily?

What we're after is a new, sustainable formula for success that allows you to embrace everything you are today. We make a huge number of choices on a day-to-day basis that determine how successful we are, and it is up to you to recognise this. Tapping into your feeling of success every day will keep you motivated and inspired.

Examples of what success may mean to you:

- ➤ Success means freedom of choice in my daily life.
- ➤ Success is the ability to earn a living from work that I'm passionate about.
- ➤ Success means living a purposeful life.
- ➤ Success is when I approve of myself and what I'm doing each day.

✱ *Remember and own your proudest moments.*

✱ *Success means living the life I choose.*

Success means living the life I choose. When I take responsibility, I feel successful every day. I've structured my diary and chosen how busy I am, how many times I've said 'yes', how fit I am, what I'm eating and how I'm spending time with my family and friends. I've also structured time for stillness, mindfulness and space, made sure my finances are up to date and worked on my business so my time is used profitably. This gives me a great sense of freedom.

YOUR DEFINITION OF SUCCESS

SUMMARY

—

{ The foundation for success }

1   Always come back to the basics.
2   Check in with who you are.
3   Discover what is true, good and possible
     about yourself.
4   Take note of the lessons you've learned.
5   Be aware of your values when making decisions.
6   Treasure golden moments daily.
7   Be true to your own definition of success.

{ Words to ponder }

1   Celebrate the little things.
2   Forgive your past mistakes.
3   Be proud of who you are.
4   Know your definition of success.
5   Be clear on your daily purpose.
6   Use your senses to notice the special
     moments in life.
7   Choose to be happy with what you have.
8   You can be who you want to be.

TIPS AND TRICKS

—

➤ Write down your values and definition of success and put them where you can see them daily.

➤ Program your values into your smartphone/computer as well.

➤ Whenever you feel too busy and out of control, go back to the basics. Revisiting your values daily will help you make informed decisions.

➤ Know your definition of success for the day ahead so that your intentions are clear.

➤ Don't get out of bed in the morning until you have gone through your purpose for the day and taken a deep breath.

➤ Tap into the feeling of when you were at your best and recreate that feeling in your body before you get up in the morning.

➤ Choose your attitude for the day.

➤ Acknowledge your golden moment, your 'rose' of the day, each night.

➤ Make a pact with yourself to be YOU Incorporated and no-one else.

True success stems from how we feel now.

SIMPLIFY

—

Beauty of style and harmony and grace and good rhythm depend on simplicity.

—

Plato

SIMPLIFY

—

Simplicity is one of the most valuable, yet underrated qualities you can strive to embrace in your life. Simplifying your life gives you clarity, freedom from unnecessary effort and the ability to be fully present. When you do this, you effectively clear your mind so you can continue on your journey feeling confident and motivated.

After exploring the first section of the book, you now know your values and purpose, and when you're at your best. You've also identified the lessons you've already learnt, the golden moments that pull you forward and your definition of success. You've created a foundation for your life.

The next step is to create a structure that will support your success. This means getting back to basics: clearing the clutter, deleting the drainers and setting some boundaries so that the obstacles we all encounter don't bring your dreams crashing down.

Simplicity brings clarity

1   When you simplify your life, you stop wasting your precious energy.

2   The clarity this brings reduces ambiguity and eliminates doubt.

3   You then have the space and opportunity to set and achieve the goals that matter most to you.

---

*   *Simplicity represents clarity, presence and freedom from effort.*

What drains you?

Is your life full of clutter? We are living in the age of time famine and digital overload, and the expectation to be 'on' constantly means there has never been a more important time for us to decompress, declutter and recalibrate our minds and bodies to ensure our wellbeing.

High achievers often struggle with feeling cluttered, overwhelmed and overextended, because they take on a lot of commitments. Working parents know only too well how difficult it is to juggle work, life and play. But really, no-one is immune to the burden of being mentally cluttered: the barista at your local cafe may be chatting politely as he foams your latte, but he's also wondering whether he should move in with his girlfriend, thinking about his plans for the weekend, wondering if he can afford to go to a music festival next month . . . and don't those concert tickets go on sale tomorrow?

Drainers aren't things we think about consciously, but are tasks in our subconscious. Decluttering your life helps eliminate them, creating a simpler, more streamlined environment. This is the big clean-out you'll need to do before you can structure the new opportunities and strategies that support you to be your best, with optimal wellness in every part of your life.

CLEARING THE DRAINERS

Many people are surprised to realise how much satisfaction they can derive from doing small, seemingly inconsequential tasks, such as putting all their gadget chargers in one place, booking a check-up with the dentist or filing documents in their correct folders. These types of tasks may not seem like big priorities, but when they are left undone they can take up mental space and chip away at your everyday focus.

By making small adjustments to your routine, you can create space within your life to manage and create everything you want to achieve. These adjustments can be anything from getting out your clothes for the following day before you go to sleep at night to setting up automatic reminders in your phone to book in repeat appointments, like medical check-ups and haircuts. Clearing your drainers has a massive positive impact on your energy and your confidence, as you'll experience the satisfaction of accomplishing something – especially if you remember to celebrate all of the wins, big and small, along the way.

{ DRAINERS }

Drainers are like tiny sandbags that are stacked at the back of your neck. Each sandbag on its own may be small and insignificant, but when they're combined they weigh you down and make you feel tired, lethargic, stressed and chaotic. Your personal environment, finances, relationships and wellbeing are the key areas where you need to simplify and eliminate drainers.

Identifying
your drainers

Think about the following aspects of your life – whenever your answer to a question is 'no', this indicates a drainer. Work to make all your answers 'yes'.

1. PERSONAL ENVIRONMENT
- ➤ Is your living space clean and inspiring?
- ➤ Is your wardrobe tidy and are all of your clothes clean, pressed and in good repair?
- ➤ Have you cleaned out your storage space and thrown away anything you haven't used in two years?
- ➤ Do you have fresh air and comfort in your home?
- ➤ Are your bed, pillow and bedding clean, comfortable and conducive to a good night's sleep?

2. FINANCES
- ➤ Do you have a budget or know your cost of living?
- ➤ Do you pay your bills on time or make arrangements with creditors?
- ➤ Are all of your receipts, invoices and financial records filed and in order?
- ➤ Do you have an automatic savings plan to save at least 10 per cent of your income?
- ➤ Do you pay off your credit card debt in full each month?

3. RELATIONSHIPS
- ➤ Do you tidy any loose ends with your partner, parents, siblings and friends by having open, honest and authentic conversations?

- ➤ Do you let the people you love know how important they are to you?
- ➤ Have you let go of any relationships that drag you down or damage you?
- ➤ Do you make requests rather than complaints?
- ➤ Do you respond to phone calls, letters and emails promptly, even if your response is brief?

4. WELLBEING

- ➤ Does your diet include fresh fruit and vegetables, and provide you with enough energy?
- ➤ Do you avoid excess tea, coffee and alcohol?
- ➤ Do you exercise for 30 minutes at least three times per week?
- ➤ Do you get enough sleep at least five nights a week?
- ➤ Do you have a holiday at least once a year?

5. FUN/CREATIVITY

- ➤ Do you invest in personal development?
- ➤ Do you laugh every day?
- ➤ Do you have a hobby?
- ➤ Do you plan regular fun activities with your partner, family and friends?
- ➤ Do you dream big dreams and work on realistic ways to make them happen?

---

* *Clear the clutter. Delete the drainers. Get clarity.*

Clutter

Clutter can make you feel stuck. When it accumulates in your living space it really has an effect on your state of mind, reminding you of all those things you mean to get around to, but somehow never do. They add up in your mind until suddenly there are just too many and the result is that none of them get done. Clutter makes it hard to relax and feel motivated at home, and it can even affect your social life if you're too embarrassed to have people over.

QUICK CLUTTER FIXES

➤ Declutter paper – books/magazines/filing.
➤ Mantra of one new thing in, one old thing out.
➤ Clean up one room at a time.
➤ If you take it off, hang it up.
➤ If you open it, close it.
➤ If you use it, clean it.

HOW TO STAY CLUTTER-FREE

➤ Review your list of drainers monthly.
➤ Aim to move each answer from 'no' to 'yes'.
➤ Diarise time to maintain your personal environment, finances, relationships and wellbeing.
➤ Create a system to achieve all of the tasks you've set yourself to clear the drainers from your life.

＊ *Do not underestimate the satisfaction that can be derived from doing small, seemingly inconsequential tasks.*

Is technology working for you?

Technology was supposed to make our lives easier, faster and more efficient. How's it working out for you?

I regularly dedicate some time to thinking about my technology strategy and whether it is working. Is technology causing me stress? Is it robbing me of my time and ability to succeed? Is it affecting my personal relationships and making it harder to renew myself?

Ideally, we should control the flow of information that comes to us, rather than it controlling us. Constant access to technology has been found to deprive us of sleep, health, relationships, space and our sense of achievement. We are addicted to information delivered at the touch of a button whenever we like, increasingly putting us in the passenger seat of life and distracting us from who we truly are and what our purpose is. When we are tuned in all the time, we lose the ability to really focus on one thing and do it well; we are partially present in life. Is that how you want to live? Having your own plan to make technology work for you is the key to using it to enhance, rather than deplete, the life you want to live.

For instance, having phones on the table during dinner does not improve either the conversation or our sense of connection. Seeing pictures of other people on Facebook or Instagram can decrease our confidence when we consider ourselves or our lifestyle in comparison. On the other hand, setting reminders and alerts so you don't have to remember everything yourself is very useful, as are mindfulness and health apps, downloads that you can listen to on the commute to work and of course smartphones make it much easier to stay in touch with people. Think about the way you use technology and make whatever adjustments are necessary to ensure it's to your advantage.

GET INTO THE DRIVER'S SEAT

Use your smartphone to help you simplify and declutter your mental space. Do this by programming alerts to take your supplements or medication at the same time each morning, or prompts every couple of hours to drink water, stand up and stretch your legs. Program reminders for things you need to do later in the day, like taking out money to pay your cleaner, buying milk on the way home after work or returning library books in your lunch break. Your phone can keep track of the important tasks and also cover the basics so that you don't have to remember everything.

{ QUICK TIPS }

➤ **No phone in the bedroom or at meals.**

➤ **When you're out with friends, have a rule that whoever spends time on their phone pays the bill.**

➤ **Program your phone/computer to work for you.**

➤ **Program your phone not to receive emails from 8 p.m. to 7 a.m.**

➤ **Program it to remind you of your own values.**

➤ **Never walk into your home, or your family or friends' homes, while you're on the phone; finish your conversation before you walk in the door.**

➤ **Ensure you have at least 1 hour of family time each day where all the phones are switched off.**

How do you declutter your habits?

It's estimated we spend up to 40 per cent of our day on habits, many of which we don't even know we have. That's a lot of time to waste on unnecessary actions that are not doing anything to move you towards the success you crave.

You can declutter your habits and create the life you want by choosing to develop habits that support your values and who you are. It's important to know that all habits run on a simple loop of:

- ➤ **Cue** – this could be a time, person, place or situation that sets your habit/s off.
- ➤ **Routine** – what the habit actually involves.
- ➤ **Reward** – the pay-off for doing it.

In order to declutter your habits, first you need to identify them and recognise the cues that kick them off. Then, think about which habits you would like to stop and ensure you avoid the cues that get them started. To create new, more constructive habits, think about how you spend the first hour of your day and see if you can build them into this time. What is your strategy to get going on the right foot each morning? How do you cue up the behaviour? What's your routine? What's the pay-off?

---

* *Habits and attitude determine most of your success.*

Make new,
better habits

Creating better habits for yourself can introduce lots of positivity to your day-to-day life. As with so many things, writing them down helps make them a reality. Ask yourself the following questions:

- ➤ Which of your current habits align with the success you want to create in your life? What are the cues, routines and rewards these habits follow?
- ➤ Which of your current habits undermine the success you want to create in your life? Can you change their cues and rewards to redirect your energy towards the outcomes you want to achieve?
- ➤ Are there any new habits you'd like to introduce? How can you cue these habits up? What will you do to create a routine? What are ways to reward yourself that are healthy and aligned to your values?

Some examples of new, better habits could be:

- ➤ Get up and move it – move your body more often for the physical and mental benefits, not to mention enjoyment!
- ➤ Meditate – take a moment, or 10 minutes if you can, to centre yourself every day.
- ➤ Rehydrate – avoid the lethargy and inability to concentrate that comes with dehydration. Buy a nice refillable water bottle and take it everywhere with you, and keep a large jug of water on your desk at work. Aim for 6–8 cups a day.
- ➤ Refuel – put wholesome, nutritious energy into your body to avoid the mood swings that come with sugar highs and lows, and keep your body functioning at its optimal level.
- ➤ Prepare yourself for the following day before going to bed.

THINGS I'D LIKE TO START DOING ON A REGULAR BASIS

1 ....

2 ....

3 ....

4 ....

5 ....

6 ....

7 ....

8 ....

9 ....

10 ....

Where are your boundaries?

Feeling overwhelmed? Taken on too much? Having trouble saying 'no'? The key to creating a more balanced life is to set boundaries that support your visions, your goals and the way you function at your best. Boundaries provide a valuable structure for communicating with those around you, at work and at play, so that everyone achieves their desired outcome without feeling frustrated or resentful. But first, you need to know where your boundaries are.

So, when should you say 'no'? Cheryl Richardson, author of *The Art of Extreme Self-Care*, suggests you create your own 'absolute' list to set boundaries for your optimal life.

What is an absolute 'yes' in your life?

What is an absolute 'no' in your life?

Learning to say 'no' is liberating and brings us back to being true to ourselves. Try practising saying 'no' in the mirror a few times until you sound clear, calm and confident.

POLITE WAYS TO SAY 'NO'

Many people, especially women, struggle to say 'no' for fear of sounding rude. But it is a vital skill that stops you committing to things that drain you and don't add anything positive to your life. Here are some suggestions for polite ways to say 'no':

- ➤ I'm swamped right now, but please ask me again another time. (If you'd like to do it at a later date.)
- ➤ I can't do it, but I can recommend someone else.
- ➤ I'd love to help, but I'd be letting other people down and I just can't do that.
- ➤ I'm sorry to disappoint you, but I promised myself I would say 'no' to things when I'm feeling overloaded.

EXAMPLE: BOUNDARIES AT WORK

Martin found that if he completed his most important tasks in the morning, he could make himself more available to his colleagues in the afternoon. To achieve this, he always started with the hardest task first. He also set the boundary that when his office door was closed, his colleagues weren't allowed to enter unless their request was urgent, and if it was open, they had to knock before entering.

EXAMPLE: BOUNDARIES AT HOME

Darcy recognised that his partner and family were the most important people in his life. He decided that between 6 p.m. and 9 p.m. each evening, he would be engaged with them, so he didn't check his phone or emails during this time. He also consciously entered the house each evening with a smile and positive energy, so he would inspire, rather than drain them. Darcy changed his family dynamic with these commitments.

EXAMPLE: BOUNDARIES FOR YOURSELF

By making one basic health commitment to yourself, such as giving up or limiting alcohol or coffee, you can bring about a huge positive change. Sally lost 4 kg in six months simply by giving up soft drinks.

---

* *We are only busy with those things we say 'yes' to.*
* *Set boundaries that support your visions and goals, and the way you function at your best.*

Characteristics of successful people

What sets successful people apart? High achievers have been found to possess certain characteristics that are integral to success. Whatever your goals in life, if you develop the characteristics of an ambitious person, you'll make progress towards your outcomes and have more chance of success.

Consider the experience of elite athletes. They obviously have an innate skill in their chosen sport, but they weren't born performing at an Olympic standard. They worked hard to develop their skills, because they possessed certain characteristics – drive, persistence, passion, determination – that helped them get up at 4 a.m. each day to train for 6 hours a day, 6 days a week.

WHAT'S YOUR OPPORTUNITY?

Do you have the characteristics of success? Review the following list and see where your approach might need a little fine-tuning to ensure you are doing what you need to create the life you most want to live.

When going through this process with me, Olympic runner Benita Johnson realised that although running was her passion, it had taken over her life. She ran too much and had lost her love for it. She had no vision for her life outside of sport, so I helped her build a new routine that supported a full, inspiring, balanced lifestyle. 'I never believed I could achieve so much while being an elite athlete!' she told me. 'I feel confident in all areas of my life now and look forward to an exciting future – as an athlete and beyond.'

---

* *Sometimes the answer to success is identifying the simple characteristic that is needed.*

WINNERS' LIST: 11 CHARACTERISTICS OF SUCCESS

1   Having a vision that's complete, inspiring, balanced and exciting.

2   Having a well-thought-out plan that backs up their vision and also takes their wellbeing into account.

3   Working hard – high-level success starts with the recognition that hard work pays off.

4   Having knowledge or training, and being committed to adapting and growing continually to improve their skills.

5   Eagerness to learn – winners study, ask questions, read and research, then apply what they learn.

6   Persistence – many people give up after their first rejection, but winners look for other opportunities to reach their outcome.

7   Taking responsibility – they know that when they blame others for their actions, they disempower themselves.

8   Networking – they value people and relationships, and their contact lists are full of people who put a high value on their friendship.

9   Making decisions where others procrastinate.

10 Self-reliance – taking the initiative and accepting the responsibilities of success.

11 Living in the present – successful people don't waste time; they use it and complete their tasks mindfully.

SUMMARY

—

We need to simplify and declutter to regain control of our lives. It is not that hard, but it takes a plan and some action without procrastination.

Drainers occur daily when we let our guard down – the mess comes in, the new purchases arrive, the information never seems to stop. Having your own plan of how to stay decluttered and operate simply and effectively is critical for long-term success.

{ **Simplify for success** }

1   Get clarity on what drains you physically, mentally and emotionally.
2   Take control of technology in your life.
3   Structure and program technology to work for you and serve you.
4   Know your habits. Work with them, change them and challenge them.
5   Set clear and simple boundaries.
6   Know when and how to say 'no', so you have time to do the things that matter the most.
7   Be aware of your success characteristics and focus on those that need improving. ›

{ Words to ponder }

1 Get excited by the fact that less is best.
2 Clutter is clog.
3 Energy is created by simplifying.
4 Love a simple life.
5 Change my habits so they work for me.
6 Get more organised.
7 Boundaries offer support.
8 This is my life and I am the driver.
9 Don't think about it; just do it.
10 Learn to say 'no'.
11 Is technology working for me or against me?
12 Tune out sometimes to be fully present in life.
13 Hard work pays off.
14 Be decisive and persistent.

TIPS AND TRICKS

—

- Declutter at least one thing each day. For instance, you might start with a wardrobe, then a bookshelf, then an office drawer, and so on.

- Donate old work clothing to charities such as Dress For Success, which supplies professional work clothes to the unemployed.

- Tidy up your work desk and keep it as clear as possible.

- Set up your technology so it works for you, not the other way around.

- Program new, good habit reminders into your phone.

- Create an automatic debit system to fast-track a savings plan.

- Use tools to limit social media use. There are programs and apps that can block the internet at certain times of the day to give you a break.

- Practise saying 'no' calmly and confidently.

- If you need to say 'no' to someone, write down a polite 'no' statement and practise it out loud so you're clear about what to say, rather than hoping the right thing will come out during the conversation.

- Look at your drainers list and identify the 'no' conversations you need to have, even with yourself (such as, 'No thanks, I can't afford it.').

- Start each day with a habit for success.

- Put out cues the night before for how you want to start your day – a healthy breakfast, the dog lead, a candle for morning meditation.

- Be in charge of your boundaries.

- Identify and eliminate the drainers in your life, one by one.

- Design boundaries at home to nurture and protect home life, and carve out quality time without distractions.

- Design boundaries at work to limit unproductive time, especially meetings and petty politicking.

Simplicity is the ultimate sophistication.

—

Leonardo da Vinci

3

STRETCH

—

The grand essentials of happiness are: something to do, something to love, and something to hope for.

—

George Washington Burnap

STRETCH

—

It is time to get creative and envision your story for the future. I do this with the help of a 'vision board', a visual representation of how I'd like my life to look. Every year I redo my vision board and revisit where I am, what I have put my energy into and what possibilities are next. I update it with new pictures, quotes and words to focus on, and it is my treasure map to guide my next steps. It gives me purpose, clarity, direction and confidence. It keeps me motivated and inspired, and challenges me to stretch beyond a place of comfort.

The result of this simple practice over the past ten years has been a deepening knowledge of my desires, a greater sense of satisfaction and joy as life unfolds, and a growing sense of achievement. I can comfortably say 'no', my boundaries are clear and everything is driven towards my core values. It is my map to fall back on when life takes unexpected twists.

Vision boards are also great fun to put together. Positive images pull us forward into new possibilities that fuel us with hope, put us on the road to finding solutions and help us realise that we have the power to make things happen in our lives. A clear vision helps you communicate your intentions to yourself and motivates you to start acting accordingly. After all, how are you going to get where you want to go if you have no idea what success actually looks like?

To get in the driver's seat of your life, you need to know where you're heading; without a clear vision, you make yourself life's passenger. This section is about stretching yourself, stirring up your creative side and mapping your hopes to create the life you most want to live. The goal is to think of exciting possibilities for what could be and to discover the greatest destination for yourself.

never
get so
busy making
a living
that you
forget to
make
a Life

Where will you be three years from now?

Three years is 156 weeks, 1095 days or 1,577,836 minutes. What could you do in that time?

Most of my clients are so busy that they don't have the space to imagine their future, and they lack the tools to explore the potential of their best possible future selves. They're very clear on all the things they don't want, but when I ask them where they would like to be in three years' time there are a lot of blank faces. The problem with this approach is that when we don't take control of our own future, life tends to knock us down.

I always start this exercise by writing my age in three years' time on a piece of paper, and then the ages of my family members. Straight away I have something concrete to help me think about what this unfolding picture might look like.

Then I give myself permission to just let go. To let the past be the past for a moment. To put my doubts and worries to one side. To simply dream that if everything went as well as it could, what would my life look like three years from now?

I write down whatever comes to mind, unedited by my fears and unlimited by lack of money, skills or time. All the hopes and dreams I'm carrying for the next three years of my life are there on the page.

---

* *If we remove the restrictions we place on ourselves, we are open to more opportunities. Dream big if you want to live big.*

Here are some questions to help kickstart your thoughts:

1   If you truly lived your purpose each day, what would you
    be doing that gave your life meaning?
2   If you were at your best more frequently, how do you think
    life would feel?
3   If you acted only on your values, what would others say
    about the way you were living?
4   If your definition of success was being realised,
    what accomplishment would you be proudest of?
5   If you were mindful of the golden moments in your life,
    what would you see?

GET SPECIFIC

➤   What kind of work will you be doing? How do you feel
    about this work?
➤   How much money will you be earning? What are you doing
    with it?
➤   What's your health like? How are you getting this result?
➤   Who brings you joy in your life? How do you spend your
    time together?
➤   What are you learning? What difference does this make
    in your life?
➤   What do you do for fun? Do you have a hobby or a passion
    project? Arc you travelling?
➤   Where are you living? What makes this feel like a haven?
➤   What have you conquered emotionally?
➤   Who are your role models and mentors?
➤   How are you moving through the world? ›

EXAMPLE: JACK'S VISION

'I'm relaxing at a five-star resort in Thailand with my family, enjoying the fruits of success from a very committed year of work. I'm on a career high after landing a prestigious and lucrative promotion that I've been working towards my entire career, and I feel creatively satisfied in my work. We own a beautiful home on the water, which we're renovating, and we've just settled on our second investment property purchase. We're planning a two-month family adventure around Europe next year. My wife and I enjoy fortnightly "date nights" and weekend getaways without the kids every three to four months. I've spent the past couple of years working on my self-development as a person, and I feel happy and content with who I am, both personally and professionally. It's liberating to experience such freedom as a result of planning who I am and where I want to get to.'

EXAMPLE: KATE'S VISION

'After working full-time as a hospital nurse for many years, my partner and I have managed to pay off most of our mortgage and our kids are old enough to need less from us, so I've returned to university to pursue a higher degree in an area I've become passionate about – midwifery. I'm only working three days a week at the hospital, so while I still enjoy the adrenaline rush of a busy shift, I also have more balance in my life. As well as studying, I'm able to take more time to exercise and look after my own health, and see more of my partner and children. I do some volunteer work in the community, educating disadvantaged women on looking after their health and caring for their babies, and get a lot of satisfaction from knowing I've contributed positively to their lives. Because I've learned to prioritise myself, I'm able to give energy to others without resenting it.'

---

*   *Creating a vision and purpose is essential. Without them, you are a passenger in life.*

THE GRAND ADVENTURE

Think of your life as a grand adventure. To get creative you'll need some space and a blank page or board, and permission from yourself to just let go. Start with your mind in a place of abundance. There is such abundance in life that many of us do not see or acknowledge. When you think of all the things you have and what is around you, you are living abundantly. There are flowers, trees, fresh air and running water – so much to be grateful for. Focusing on what we already have, and the choices we can make, is a great place to start.

HOW TO CREATE YOUR THREE-YEAR VISION

- ➤ Write down your age, and the ages of your family members, in three years' time.
- ➤ Put your mind in a place of abundance. Focus on the things you already have and the choices you're free to make.
- ➤ Try to spend 15–20 minutes each day for three days in a row just writing down what you hope your life will be like three years from now.
- ➤ Be as specific and detailed as possible, so you can see, feel and hear what this new reality will be like.
- ➤ Notice which ideas you keep coming back to once you've completed this exercise.

---

* *Beware of dream stealers: people who encourage you to play it safe and make you believe you'll never reach your dreams.*

What's on your vision board?

How can you start to make your three-year vision a reality? I use my one-year vision board as a means of turning my longer-term dreams into shorter-term realities. It helps me paint a picture of the future I want to achieve, providing a daily touchpoint to inspire and guide me.

For example, if you want to be healthier, an image of the type of food you want to be eating will remind you of this each day. When you can see things, you can start feeling them, and then you can start believing in them and setting up the structures to get you there.

Creativity and visualisation are life skills that can be practised. Remember, 'like attracts like'. Whatever we focus on, we give energy to. If we focus on stress, we get more stress. If we want joy, we need to feel and acknowledge joy when it is there; if we want wellbeing, we need to feel and focus on wellbeing. What are you envisioning for the upcoming year?

Start by simply printing out pictures or cutting out images or words that inspire you from magazines. Look through books for words, quotes and affirmations that warm your heart. Think in key themes – like career, family, health, finance, fun and home – of the kind of life you wrote about creating. The more we can see, hear and feel what this vision of our future will be like, the stronger the pull to make it our reality will be. Pictures, words, symbols and colours are a great way to start tangibly creating this new reality.

There are also digital options for creating vision boards you might like to consider if you want to see yours on your smartphone or as a screensaver. Whatever process you choose, be sure you can see your vision daily to guide you forward.

---

* *Let your vision board be your gift, your light and your constant reminder of how you want to grow and evolve.*

QUESTIONS TO ASK AS YOU MAKE YOUR VISION BOARD

- ➤ Where will you be living a year from now?
- ➤ What will you be doing for work a year from now?
- ➤ Who will you be with a year from now?
- ➤ What emotions will you be feeling in a year's time?
- ➤ How will you look after your health in a year's time?
- ➤ Who will be inspiring your journey in a year's time?
- ➤ What will you be learning a year from now?
- ➤ What are you telling yourself with these pictures?
- ➤ Is this the life you most want to be living?

How active is your vision board? This is your destiny, so make it vivid, vibrant and vital. Make it count.

Once you have completed your board, hang it in a spot where you can see it daily. Mine is in my office; some people hang theirs behind their bedroom door so they wake up to it. When you see it often, you start to commit it to memory; it becomes a part of your destiny and meditation process. Let your subconscious mind continually absorb this new reality every day and night, reminding you where you are heading in life. Allow the opportunities to flow into your life, and because you know where you want to go, you will see them clearly.

My vision board represents the space I need in life, the wellbeing that is at my foundation, my relationships, my role models and the characteristics in myself that I want to develop, my house/car and other belongings, and the places I want to travel. It includes my hobbies and the feelings I want to feel, as well as the basic things I am grateful for in life. It represents my purpose, values and definition of success. It gives me the confidence, optimism and courage to create the life I most want to be living.

✱ *Success is when I approve of myself and what I am doing each day.*

Si

blessed are those
who see beautiful
things in places
others see
nothing

If you don't
imagine,
nothing ever
happens
at all

How do you
stretch yourself?

What was the last new thing you learnt? We are creatures of progress, with a lifetime's hunger for improvement. The very fact that we continue to evolve over the course of our lives is evidence of our ongoing need for growth and learning.

Yet as we get older, the chance to discover new approaches, new ideas and new wonders often fades away in the everyday business of life. But without opportunities to stretch ourselves, we soon stagnate and plateau into lives of boredom and disappointment. So, what are you learning?

I find that I learn best by listening, so I'm a big fan of audio books and podcasts. Truth is, it doesn't matter what form your learning takes, whether it's reading books, attending a formal course or public lecture, taking part in a conversation or observing an informal life lesson. The point is simply to seek opportunities that stretch us just beyond our comfort zone and offer new challenges that help us grow.

That's right: it's not enough just to absorb information, we actually need to apply what we learn to our lives to enjoy the true value of our discoveries. One of the easiest ways to do this is to think about the questions that new insights might prompt us to ask about the lives we're living.

---

* *Seek out challenges that stretch you just beyond your comfort zone and offer new opportunities for growth.*

HOW COULD I EXPERIMENT WITH THIS IDEA IN MY LIFE?

Here are some of my favourite questions to fire up my brain and get me stretching a little further:

- ➤ If there was one thing I could do based on what I've just learnt, what would it be?
- ➤ If I lived my life by this lesson, where would I be three years from now? Is this what I want?
- ➤ How might this lesson have an impact on my vision for the year ahead?
- ➤ If there was no chance of failure, what things would I be willing to try?
- ➤ What would it take to master this part of life? Am I up for it?
- ➤ Where can I learn more about this idea? Who could I talk to about it?

GOING FURTHER

Here are some more questions I like to ask myself to stretch my life vision further when I feel things have become too comfortable:

- ➤ If I were to fully live my life and feel a holistic sense of wellbeing, what could I do right now?
- ➤ How would I feel about adding five daring goals that really would be a stretch?
- ➤ How can I be more specific in each area of my life?
- ➤ What makes my heart sing?
- ➤ If I had all the money and success that I desire, what would I do with it?

Have you mapped your hopes?

Now you know where your life is headed in the longer term (your three-year vision) and the shorter term (your one-year vision board) and the places you might be able to stretch yourself, it's time to figure out how you'll get from where you are to where you want to go. Yes, it's time for a little reality check to see what goals you're really willing to set.

You see, while most of us believe tomorrow could be better than today, only half of us believe we can actually make it so. And this is the difference between wishing for the future we want to create and hoping for it. To have hope, we need some clear 'want-to' (rather than 'have-to') goals, pathways to move us towards these goals, and a plan to maintain our willpower to get us to the final result.

Hope is the work of your head and your heart. Not only does it lift your spirits, it also buoys your energy, makes life worthwhile and changes your day-to-day behaviour. So, what are you hoping for?

Start by identifying three to five goals you want to accomplish this year. I start by looking at my vision board and noting down some specific goals for the year ahead.

FIVE STEPS TO CLARIFY YOUR GOALS

- ➤ What are your goals in simple terms?
- ➤ Are you clear on your specific objectives?
- ➤ Why are you doing this?
- ➤ What do you really want to achieve?
- ➤ Do your goals have depth and do you really understand them? ›

Rather than thinking 'I'll be more healthy, both physically and mentally', be more specific: 'I'll do yoga at least three times a week, meditate before bed at least three times a week, and make sure every meal contains some fresh produce.' Make sure the goals you set are achievable, as there's no point in setting unrealistic goals destined for failure.

Then, try to find at least three pathways – actions you can take – to make these goals a reality. This could be booking yourself into a yoga course, putting a reminder note on your bedside table to meditate before going to sleep, and spending half an hour on Sundays to plan the food you are going to eat over the coming week. I try to think about what I'll do each day, each week, and each month to start getting the outcome I want. Again, try to be as specific as possible; so, rather than thinking 'Get more training', try 'Complete a short course learning leadership techniques.'

Next, think of at least one obstacle that may arise for each of your pathways. Perhaps working late and last-minute social occasions could disrupt your yoga. Studies have found we're more likely to reach our goals if we plan for the obstacles upfront, so be honest about what might slow you down, trip you up or make you give up completely.

Finally, write down all the things you can do to maintain your willpower as you set about making your goals a reality. How will you make the journey enjoyable? Is there someone, a friend, work colleague or family member, who can support you along the way? How will you measure your progress? What will you do to celebrate the small milestones? These details will be vital for helping you achieve the outcomes you desire.

MAKE YOUR HOPES A REALITY

➤ Carry them with you all day.

➤ Write them on your bathroom mirror in fluorescent texta.

➤ Put them alongside your vision board.

➤ Program them into your phone.

➤ Write them on a card and store it in your wallet.

➤ Copy them onto the front page of your diary or planner
so they greet you when you open it each day.

MY TIP

When setting your goals, start with your overall vision, including those big dreams and lofty pie-in-the-sky ambitions. This will help you break them down into smaller wins, with each step taking you closer to your final goal. I write down my intention and affirmation for each day in the morning, so I really focus and get that sense of achievement; no matter how small the task is, it is on track with my vision.

✱ *We're more likely to reach our goals if we plan for the obstacles upfront, so be honest about what might slow you down, trip you up or make you give up completely.*

✱ *If you don't have time to write down your goals, when are you going to find the time to accomplish them?*

EXAMPLE HOPE MAP

TOPICS	GOAL	OBSTACLE
MENTAL HEALTH	Have 1 hour a day of space.	No time, too busy.
PHYSICAL HEALTH	Eat breakfast.	Always in a rush, too tired, can't be bothered.
RELATIONSHIPS	Honest and open, supportive and generous.	Honesty can be painful at times, lack of time and energy to invest in people.
FINANCES	Pay off credit card debt.	Lack of money.
PERSONAL ENVIRONMENT	Stay tidy for clarity.	Lack of time, task is overwhelming.
CAREER	Get more clients.	Too busy to spend time looking for them.
PASSIONS/HOBBIES	Have more fun in life.	Too busy, too tired.

PATHWAY	OUTCOME
30 minutes morning meditation – get up earlier. Silence in the car. Phone ban of 1 hour when I arrive home.	Feeling of space and control in my life. Having a simple, defined rule makes it easy to achieve.
Prepare food the night before. Make it delicious so it'll be worth the effort.	More energy in the morning. Not as likely to eat unhealthy morning snacks.
Focus on who I want to be in the relationship. Stop comparing myself to others. Stay away from drainers and dream stealers.	Feel energetic and enjoy people. Attract more like-minded people when I am focusing on being the best me I can be.
Start a cost-of-living spreadsheet to record what I spend money on. Put a hold on my credit card.	Regain control of my money. Can make more informed choices that add to my confidence, rather than spending for therapy!
One-touch rule. Don't shuffle things around; put them away. When getting changed, put clothes away.	Less tidying all the time by doing the simple things as they arise and not double-handling everything.
Make one extra call per week; have a list ready to go that inspires you and keeps you aware of what the reward for your commitment will be.	Get results by making more connections and opening more doors.
Get a friend to be a hobby buddy and try three new things, such as photography, cooking or a fun run.	Enjoy new options without feeling intimidated and discover new skills to get passionate about.

YOUR HOPE MAP

TOPICS	GOAL	OBSTACLE
MENTAL HEALTH		
PHYSICAL HEALTH		
RELATIONSHIPS		
FINANCES		
PERSONAL ENVIRONMENT		
CAREER		
PASSIONS/HOBBIES		

PATHWAY	OUTCOME

SUMMARY

—

As you travel towards your vision, keep a daily journal that helps you celebrate and be grateful for the progress, big and small, that you're making each day. This simple discipline has been found to give us the energy and optimism to keep moving towards our goals.

This is one of the areas I spend a lot of time on in my life. Thinking about my vision, how I'm stretching myself, the hopes I'm focused on achieving and my sense of gratitude are how I create the incredible life I'm living. It is creative, it is fun and it keeps me focused on being me. It also helps me stay active, inspired, motivated and focused on putting energy into the things I really want for my life.

{ **Words to ponder** }

1. Live your life on purpose.
2. Visualise the feelings, thoughts and things that you want in life.
3. Allow yourself to dream.
4. Enjoy being creative.
5. Love the 'now' and the process of creation.
6. What you focus on increases.
7. Create bite-sized tasks that put you in the direction of your vision.
8. Always have a daily list of goals and intentions so you stay on track.
9. You are your own best friend.

TIPS AND TRICKS

—

- Create your vision based on your own core values.

- Decide that this is your life and you own it.

- Think three years down the track and plant seeds that will bear fruit.

- Be clear on your vision for the next twelve months and what you want to accomplish.

- Seek sources of learning and ask questions that stretch your thinking.

- Map your hopes and act accordingly.

- When you see an inspiring image or a real-life moment that really reflects who you want to be, capture it on your smartphone and add it to your moodboard. Start a collection. It really will come in handy.

- Be specific about something you want to learn – how to do a headstand, master your phobia of public speaking or learn to speak Hebrew – then map out a specific plan to get those skills.

- Each day, program reminders into your smartphone that include actions you need to take to achieve goals, like run 10 kilometres in preparation for the half-marathon, transfer $100 to your credit card to stay on target for eliminating debt or organise a 'date night' for next Saturday.

- Remember to keep tasks bite-sized! Break them down so you can make smart, steady progress.

- Keep your vision board and goals visible. A plan that gets filed away will be forgotten with the endless distractions of day-to-day life.

- Think about the 'dream stealers' in your life. Who are they and how will you limit their negative impact on your life plans?

- Practise gratitude – find ways to add gratitude into the everyday. Create cues for moments when you'll consciously identify what you are grateful for. This could be while you're waiting at traffic lights, as you sip your first cup of tea for the day, as you begin a workout or while putting on your make-up.

If you want to build a ship, don't drum up people to collect wood and don't assign them tasks and work, but rather teach them to long for the endless immensity of the sea.

—

Antoine de Saint-Exupéry

STRUCTURE

—

The time which we have at our disposal every day is elastic; the passions that we feel expand it, those that we inspire contract it; and habit fills up what remains.

—

Marcel Proust

STRUCTURE

—

It is exciting to start this part of the journey and I suggest that you keep revisiting this chapter. This is the building part, the part that creates the structure to support the purpose, values and definition of success you have set so that you can make your vision a reality, keep stretching yourself and realise your hopes. This is where the accomplishments start to kick in and where the rewards begin to pile up.

Structure also gives you some easy levers to pull each month to adjust your path as needed. The circumstances of our lives are constantly evolving and our thoughts, feelings and behaviours sometimes need to shift accordingly. Structure should always guide you, but never govern you. It should help you find the rhythm of the life you want to be living.

You're probably already pretty good at creating structures for your life, but I'll hazard a guess that while your annual holiday plans are analysed, reviewed and shared in big, bold letters on your calendar, the same attention to structure isn't present in the rest of your life. In fact, in my experience most of us spend more time planning our holidays than we do our health, finances, careers or families. Of course, there's nothing wrong with looking forward to a holiday, but if it becomes all we really have to live for each year, there's a problem!

Valuing time

It's important to value time and to understand what it is doing for you – not just when you're taking a break, but in every moment. The way you structure your activities will either give you a sense of energy, achievement, success and fulfilment, or will make you feel stressed, out of control and exhausted.

Time is a gift and it is our responsibility to 'own and drive' it. This means taking responsibility for what we want to feel (unhurried, calm and relaxed, or rushed, anxious and stressed?) and understanding the consequences of each of our activities.

Our perception of time changes according to our circumstances. Any woman in the throes of labour will tell you that 1 minute is a very long time. Consider how a 15-minute block of time feels when you're in the following situations:

➤ On a freeway in bumper-to-bumper traffic, with no music and no passengers.
➤ Running late for an appointment or meeting.
➤ In a slow-moving queue at the bank, post office or supermarket.
➤ Waiting for someone who is running late for an appointment with you.
➤ Sipping cocktails on a relaxing holiday.
➤ Deeply immersed in reading a book, watching a film or doing your favourite hobby. ›

DO YOU NEED MORE TIME?

Are you experiencing a 'time famine' – the feeling that you'll never have enough time, no matter how fast you're running? Does this sound familiar to you?

Leslie Perlow of Harvard Business School in the US is a specialist in organisational behaviour. Her research indicates that feeling as though we're experiencing a time famine has very real consequences, from increased stress to diminished satisfaction with our lives. But unfortunately, we're often too busy taking action to really think through the importance of what we're doing.

The good news is that we can also create a situation where we feel 'time affluent', with all the time we need entirely within our reach. All it takes is the willingness to structure our time around doing the things that really matter and letting go of the idea that our level of busyness somehow defines our level of importance.

Let's change our thinking and embrace planning to focus on the activities that truly make a difference, so we can create the kind of freedom we long for in our lives.

Structure

=

Balance and Control

=

Freedom

Planning ahead

Now you have your hopes mapped out, what will the month ahead look like? Start your planning by writing down a list of what you need to do. You might like to use colour pens, coloured paper or a new diary or smartphone app – be creative and make it special so that the very idea of planning feels more exciting and enjoyable. As the month progresses and you make your way through the list, tick things off or cross them out because this gives your brain a lovely hit of dopamine, one of the feelgood chemicals our bodies produce that will help you increasingly look forward to making plans and carrying them out.

QUICK TIPS TO GET STARTED

➤ Invest in a diary or smartphone app that gives you an annual, monthly and weekly view of your priorities.

➤ Make sure your diary or app is something you love and will be excited about using.

➤ Play around with the diary or app to find the way it works best for you.

➤ Make this diary or app your touchstone throughout the day to guide what you do.

➤ Give yourself the pleasure of ticking things off!

---

* *Structure is a powerful and highly underrated tool that will fundamentally change your life for the better.*

Want to go
with the flow?

The world's most effective leaders understand that forward planning is essential for success. By loosely planning each year in advance, month by month, you'll be well prepared for the busy times, but also able to factor in plenty of fun.

An annual calendar puts you in charge of how you use your time. It gives you the perspective and focus you need to move from the passenger seat to the driver's side of life. It's the next step in bringing your purpose, vision and hope map to life.

FIVE STEPS TO PLAN YOUR YEAR
Start with the obvious and jot down birthdays, holidays and other regular significant events that are part of the rhythm of your life. Don't get bogged down in small details yet – focus on the big-ticket occasions that shape your year.

1 **Add your hopes**
   Looking at your hope map, are there key milestones, events or opportunities you want to note? For example, the date of the marathon you want to run, a conference you want to attend or the go-live date of a major project.

2 **Bust the energy drainers**
   Add any known energy drainers that will have to be taken care of, so you're prepared to tackle these head-on. For example, when will you do your annual tax return, service the car, spring-clean your living space?

3   **Prioritise some fun**
    Plan some pick-me-ups in your calendar to keep your
    motivation and energy levels up. For example, have you
    booked an annual holiday, is there a concert you want
    to see, would you value a spa day with a friend?

4   **Breathe**
    Take a deep breath and relax, knowing this list is there to
    guide you, not govern you, as you focus on the things you
    most want to complete.

Of course, if your annual calendar looks overwhelming at this
point, now is a good time to see what you can delegate, what you can
delay until next year or what you can simply delete. Be sure that when
you look at the big picture of what will unfold this year, it is taking you
towards the kind of success you want.

---

*   *Think of this as your road map for life. You're eliminating the dead-ends and
     wrong turns, and taking the fastest, most direct route to your destination.*

Do you know what this month will bring?

Personal fulfilment depends on how you value each and every moment. Now that you have planned your year, as each month approaches it's time to get more specific about what you want to achieve, the time you need to unwind and the golden moments you want to create. To create your monthly plan (see page 110), first write down the key activities on your annual planner that occur in the coming month. Now, add:

➤ **Personal priorities**
Book in personal time in the same way you would schedule a meeting. For example, my family's first hour at home each evening is our most important meeting of the day. Do you need to plan time with your family, your partner or your friends?

➤ **Health and wellbeing**
Exercise, food, fun and time out are vital and should be shaped around your work.

➤ **Hopes**
What do you need to focus on doing this month so that you can move forward on your path?

➤ **Energy drainers**
What are the drainers you need to take care of this month? Haircuts, gardening, paying the bills?

➤ **Mental breathing space**
Make time for rest and recovery, when you can just hang out and be. I love my couch nights!

When you've finished drawing up your plan for the month, step back and take a look at the big picture once again. Is this the kind of month you want to be living? Is it moving you towards your purpose, vision and hopes? Are you looking forward to the month unfolding? If the answer is 'no' to any of these, put yourself in the driver's seat and find a way to change the direction, shift gears or make the journey more enjoyable. This is your life; you need to make conscious choices about the way you live to achieve the outcomes you most desire.

Seeing a month mapped out in advance is liberating and keeps us focused and inspired. Here is an example of a template my clients use to help them plan each month.

SAMPLE MONTHLY PLAN	
HEALTH AND WELLBEING	➤ Exercise, including when I will run, lift weights, stretch, go to yoga. ➤ Massages and listening to inspirational and interesting downloads.
PERSONAL PRIORITIES	➤ Date nights, time with the kids, time with extended family, and some fun time and dinners with friends.
HOPES	➤ The outcomes I want to achieve and progress I'd like to make at work. ➤ The personal goals I am working towards.

YOUR MONTHLY PLAN

KEY ACTIVITIES	
PERSONAL PRIORITIES	
HEALTH AND WELLBEING	
HOPES	
ENERGY DRAINERS	
MENTAL BREATHING SPACE	

Your time is limited, so don't waste it living someone else's life.

—

Steve Jobs

Can you fit everything in?

Looking at your monthly plan, you might be wondering how you'll fit everything in. After all, there are only 24 hours in a day and yet there's so much living to be done.

The good news, as we discovered earlier, is that studies have found most of us spend almost half our day in a haze of habits we may not even be fully aware of. I'm not suggesting we try to claw back all that time, but what if we could be more mindful about how our habits are playing out and use the simple habit loop we discovered earlier of cue, routine and reward to prioritise some of the changes we want most?

CREATING A WEEKLY HABIT MAP

1   The best place to start is by creating a map of your week and noting down the key success habits you already have. For example, do you already have an exercise routine, do you have a regular meditation time, do you spend time with your family each evening, and so on? What are the habits that already exist in your week to bring your purpose, values, vision and hopes to life? And when do they happen? Write these on your weekly map.

2   Are there other habits you'd like to add to make your most desired behaviours a sure thing? These don't have to be big investments of energy or time; you'll be amazed at what you can accomplish in as little as 10 minutes. For example, if one of your hopes is to spend more time catching up with friends, a 10-minute habit of calling or writing to someone first thing each night after dinner can have you touching base with up to thirty people each month. Or, if one of your hopes is to learn more about a new topic, a 10-minute habit

of reading a book or article each morning before you turn on your computer at work can have you quickly gaining more knowledge. What are the small habits you'd like to create in your week to start prioritising the changes you want to see in your life? When will these habits take place and how can you get started? How will you celebrate what you've done so that you'll want to do it again tomorrow? Add these to your weekly map.

3   Pay particular attention to your morning and evening routines – you want to start the day with power and finish with a good night's sleep.

4   Make weekly diary planning a habit so you can keep moving towards the outcomes you want. At each weekly update, tick off the things you've achieved – this gives you a sense of accomplishment and boosts your confidence.

Will these habits stick? Are they realistic? Do they fit in with your work hours and your family commitments? Will you still have time for rest and recovery?

Don't set yourself up for failure. Start with small changes, just one at a time, and when a habit begins to stick, add the next one. And then the next one. And then the next one, until you feel that your weeks are truly being spent in the ways you find most rewarding.

---

*   *It is important to value time and to understand what it is doing for you – not just when you are taking a break, but at each and every moment.*

Will you make today count?

One of the commitments I urge all my clients to make is to keep a daily diary. This is the moment when all the annual, monthly and weekly habit plans come together into one clear set of daily actions.

Not having a diary is an act of self-sabotage – it's like charging expenses on your credit card all month, not keeping tabs on your spending, never asking for receipts, and then complaining about how high your credit card bill is.

While many people have moved to electronic diaries in recent years, I've found lots of my clients are switching back to paper options. The old saying 'don't think it, ink it' seems to be more important than ever. Personally, I don't think it matters which approach you use as long as you are driving it, it is working for you and you are getting the results and sense of satisfaction you need to stay motivated.

At the start of each week, use your monthly planner and weekly habit map to complete your daily diary. Be sure to note:

➤ Significant moments and milestones
➤ Meetings for work, home or play
  (with time for travel if required)
➤ Times for your habits
➤ Key actions you need to take to help
  fulfil your hopes
➤ Energy drainers you need to take care of

Be generous in your allocation of time so you're not running from one activity to the next and driving yourself crazy.

Remember the 80:20 rule. Life moves constantly; a reasonable balance to aim for is knowing that you can probably control 80 per cent of your time, while 20 per cent of the time you'll be thrown a curve ball. Leave space for the curve balls so they don't send you into chaos and overwhelm you.

FIVE QUESTIONS TO GUIDE YOUR DIARY PLANNING

1   Will I feel that this was a day I lived well?
2   Will this move me towards my purpose, vision, values and hopes?
3   Have I made quality time for the people who are most important to me?
4   What are the rewards and consequences?
5   Have I structured calm and balance into my life by using my success toolkit (see page 145)?

---

*   *Depth and fulfilment in life depend on how you value each and every moment.*
*   *Not having a diary is an act of self-sabotage.*

Where will you start?

My favourite book is *Eat That Frog!* by Brian Tracy. I've found it to be extremely practical when it comes to getting things done. The concept is that the frog is the biggest and most important task of the day, the one you usually procrastinate on. So to start the day, you discipline yourself to 'eat the frog' and do this task immediately, completing it before moving on to anything else. 'Eat the frog' is my morning motto and is programmed into my phone.

Self-managing means setting yourself a structure to carry out tasks, such as 'eat the frog'. People often find it easy to plan, but they have to carry it through by executing the new habits they need to put in place and finishing what they set out to do. Brian Tracy says there are three 'D's to address when forming new habits: decision, discipline and determination. When I'm trying to create new habits to assist with my self-managing, I find it helps to visualise myself as the person I intend to be and that the job is done.

As you can imagine, I have a list a mile long of dreams, ideas, things to do, and a business and family to run. Part of my self-managing is realising that there needs to be an underlying aim of total wellbeing for myself. I find that if I am fit, healthy and well, and have had enough sleep and nutritious food, I can ensure my family, my business and everybody else are getting the best from me.

---

*   *I build my self-motivation through confidence, positive thinking, focus and a motivating environment.*

Who is on your team?

Wanting to do something and actually doing it can be two very different things. The distinction between people who never reach their goals and those who achieve one goal after another often comes down to the ability to self-motivate. Motivation is your internal drive to achieve, produce, develop, evolve and keep moving towards your goals.

Motivation is linked to your level of initiative in setting challenging goals for yourself, and your belief that you have the skills and abilities required to achieve these goals. You can boost your motivation in the following ways:

1 **Confidence**
   This makes you resilient and driven, viewing difficult goals as challenging rather than impossible. You're more likely to bounce back from setbacks and believe in your ability to succeed.

2 **Realistic optimism**
   This is particularly important when things aren't going as planned or unexpected setbacks arise. Don't think 'I knew I couldn't do it,' but 'This one failure isn't going to stop me.'

3 **Focus**
   Setting clear, strong goals helps you stay focused, as does recognising your achievements.

4 **Support**
   Surround yourself with people who remind you of your goals and encourage your progress, and are willing to celebrate your success. Seek out resources that will support you. ›

YOUR DREAM TEAM

Identifying your dream team and keeping these people around you is an important part of your toolkit and structure for success. Your dream team may include:

- ➤ Role models
- ➤ Mentors
- ➤ Friends
- ➤ Coaches
- ➤ Personal trainers
- ➤ Family
- ➤ Colleagues
- ➤ Your own mastermind group of like-minded people
- ➤ An exercise buddy

You can also find motivation in different tools, such as:

- ➤ Books and audiobooks
- ➤ Magazines
- ➤ Music
- ➤ Podcasts
- ➤ Public talks (such as TED talks)
- ➤ Gratitude journals

Plan your dream team into your life. For example, whenever I go for a walk on my own I listen to an inspirational audiobook. I set up a monthly coffee date with my mastermind group, see my life coach once a month, and go walking with my fitness buddy once a week. Every night I alternate between writing a gratitude journal entry and listening to a meditation in bed.

What we think,
or what we know,
or what we believe,
is of little consequence.
The only consequence
is what we do.

—

John Ruskin

Are you committed enough?

When you are truly committed to your goals, you achieve them. When you don't achieve them, the problem is that your level of commitment isn't high enough. In every moment of your life you are committed to something – you may be lying on the couch watching television, thinking you're not committed to anything, but lying on the couch and watching television is exactly what you are committed to doing.

Our commitment to something can be influenced by an even stronger underlying commitment. These can have both a positive and negative face. For example, being independent can be a wonderful thing, but it can also be a hindrance in some aspects of your life. Working out an optimal balance is about identifying what you are truly committed to. Following through on commitments is very powerful, as it builds your confidence and builds trust with those around you.

Think of each task on your 'to do' list or in your diary and consider where it fits on your scale of commitment. Has it been sitting there for months, waiting for you to 'find the time'? Which of these levels of commitment are you operating at?

1 Hmm...
2 I'll think about it.
3 I'll do it (unless something comes up).
4 I'll do it (unless something important comes up).
5 I'll drag myself there bloodied and broken if I have to.

For example, if Martin says, 'I'll try to quit smoking this weekend,' he really means that he is not ready to commit to quitting and hasn't fully explored the commitments that smoking fulfils. By using the word 'try' he can avoid quitting and exploring what his commitment to smoking actually means. This is a world away from, 'I will stop smoking on Saturday.' ›

If you're lacking the commitment to follow through on your plans, try this to find the real reasons you're getting stuck:

➤ Write down a goal or desire you've been unable to attain. For example: 'Go to the gym twice a week.'

➤ Make a list of the actions you have taken (or not taken) that are in direct opposition to this goal. For example: 'Worked longer hours, so told myself I didn't have time; stopped working out with my gym buddy and lost that accountability; eventually cancelled gym membership as I wasn't using it.'

➤ Imagine that these choices, which have taken you away from your desired goal, are an expression of a deeper commitment. Consider: 'What commitment are these choices in direct alignment with?' The underlying commitment is: 'My gym membership is expensive and I'm not getting value, so I'll cancel it and save money.'

➤ Now that you know the real reason why this underlying commitment has held you back, reset your goal and truly commit to it. For example, join a gym that offers better value and classes you really like, find cheaper or free ways to exercise such as cycling to work, walking in the park or doing yoga DVDs at home, or find a friend to work out with and re-establish motivation and accountability.

---

* *Every time you just 'try', instead of truly committing to achieving a set task, you rob yourself of time and energy (both physical and emotional).*

Will you take responsibility?

When you hear the word 'responsibility', do you associate it with a burden to carry or the opportunity to feel free?

When things don't go to plan, we often look for someone to blame, turning ourselves into victims who are resentful and powerless. When you choose to blame, you choose to burden.

But when we take responsibility for the way that our own thoughts, feelings and behaviours have contributed to a situation, it puts us back in the driver's seat and gives us the power and freedom to respond differently. If you accept the saying, 'If it's to be, it's up to me!', there's very little you can't achieve.

> ➤ **Blame** burdens us with disempowerment and loss of freedom.
> ➤ **Responsibility** frees us with power and choices.

Taking responsibility simply requires us to ask: 'What have I done to cause or affect this? What can I do now to improve the situation?'

Consider Lesley, a finance broker who, at the age of fifty-five, lost money in share investments. He was angry. He felt cheated. A large proportion of his life savings was gone and he blamed his financial advisor for giving him bad advice. He was becoming very bitter over the whole ordeal, which was holding him back from setting new financial goals for his retirement. But he'd agreed to make the investment, which was a gamble, and he needed to take responsibility for his choices.

As well as being disempowering, to blame is to dwell and hence a waste of time. And blaming yourself is just as damaging as blaming others. Instead, try to think of it as taking responsibility for the things you are responsible for, and letting go of the rest. Once you are ready to do this, you can forgive yourself or others for mistakes and move on.

Choose
to blame

=

Choose
to burden

THREE STEPS
TO GET YOUR LIFE MOVING

BLAME	*Three things I blame myself or others for:*
CAUSES	*How did I cause or contribute to the situation?*
RESOLUTION	*How can I take responsibility and improve this situation?*

How can you avoid self-sabotage?

Does fear, anxiety or worry ever get the better of your plans? You know those moments, when you unexpectedly find yourself cleaning the house, hiding on the couch or distracted by 101 other things, none of which your diary suggests you're meant to be doing right now. All of us suffer occasionally by letting our best intentions be hijacked by fear.

COMMON SELF-SABOTAGES

- ➤ Fear of success.
- ➤ Fear of failure.
- ➤ Beliefs such as 'I'm not good enough' or 'There isn't enough to go around'.
- ➤ Beliefs such as 'I'm independent – I don't need help'.
- ➤ Beliefs such as 'I don't deserve it'.

If your fears are holding you back from following through on your purpose, vision and hopes, it is time to recognise that these beliefs are simply stories we tell ourselves. Your brain is a sense-making machine and one of the ways it puts the pieces of your life together is by constantly creating stories about why things are happening and what might happen next. Sometimes these stories are accurate, but much of the time they're not. When fear is putting you in life's passenger seat, it is time to ask: 'Is there any other explanation for what's unfolding?'

Byron Katie, author of *Loving What Is*, suggests that when fear or unhappiness is holding us back, we need to do what she calls 'The Work'. It's a powerful tool that I've found gives excellent results. Take a look at her website, www.thework.com, and apply it to your fears.

✱ *Own your limiting beliefs and work to reduce them.*

Are you ready for the obstacles?

When you created your hope map (pages 86–87), you discovered the importance of planning for obstacles if you want to reach your goals. Common obstacles to wellbeing and success are:

➤ Not enough time.
➤ Not enough money.
➤ Don't like exercise.
➤ It's too hard.
➤ The timing's not right.
➤ I wouldn't know where to start.
➤ I travel too much.
➤ I don't know the right people.
➤ My family and friends would laugh.
➤ I'm no good at that.
➤ I'm too tired.
➤ If I succeed, people will expect me to keep it up.

To ensure these obstacles don't hold you back, challenge yourself to find small changes that make the outcomes you want possible.

---

* *If you are fully present with your senses, you can really live life with depth, clarity and a sense of total abundance.*

PLANNING FOR OBSTACLES

Think about the obstacles that may prevent you reaching
your goals and how you can plan ahead to overcome them.

OBSTACLE	SOLUTION
Example: Not enough time	➤ Wake up half an hour earlier and get moving. ➤ Leave work on time, by 6 p.m. ➤ Work smarter instead of harder.
Example: Too busy to cook healthy meals	➤ On Sunday, prepare meals for the week ahead. ➤ Prepare your breakfast ingredients the night before. ➤ Start your own recipe book of healthy, quick meals.

SUMMARY

—

The foundations are set, the clutter is gone, you have simplicity in what you want out of life and you know what you need to do to get there. It is now time to compile and use the tools in this chapter to make your definition of success a reality.

Creating routine and structure in your day is the key to a calm, balanced and successful life. Structure is a powerful and highly underrated tool that will *fundamentally change your life* for the better and give you the kind of time affluence you've only dreamed of.

To achieve your goals, the things that matter most in your life need to be planned and supported: health, relationships, work, money, fun and time out.

When the right structure is in place the basics are covered, so you can be spontaneous and grab new opportunities without sacrificing your normal obligations. It gives you balance and clarity, and the space and freedom you need to live a life you love. Hold these plans lightly and be guided, but not governed, by the changes you're creating.

Planning my diary annually, monthly, weekly and daily so that I can drive my habits, tackle difficult tasks and use technology to support me is the only way I can maintain my energy at an optimal level. Structure is how I ensure I have time for creativity and fun, for self-care and a good night's sleep. It allows me to stay in the driver's seat, and never return to the passenger seat.

TIPS AND TRICKS

—

Whether you use an online planner or a paper diary, spend a little time each day planning how the hours will unfold. A week-to-a-page diary is a perfect 'at a glance' representation of where you're investing your energy, and helps you ensure you're moving towards the purpose, vision, values and hopes you most want.

- ➤ Take the time to plan your year, your month and your week.
- ➤ Map your habits around the behaviours you most want to develop.
- ➤ Keep a daily diary and savour the joy of ticking things off.
- ➤ Ask yourself if you are committed to being You.
- ➤ Make sure you have a dream team of people urging you on.
- ➤ Ensure you're taking responsibility for what you can do.
- ➤ Don't allow your fears to hold you back.
- ➤ Have your obstacle plan ready and don't use excuses as a way to avoid showing up.

---

* *Remember: first we make our habits, and then our habits make us.*

Structure is the cornerstone of calmness, clarity and control.

SUCCEED

—

Opportunities multiply as they are seized.

—

Sun Tzu

SUCCEED

—

By now you have established the foundations of your purpose and values, and what success means to you. You have also simplified key areas of your life, ready to stretch forward towards your vision and hopes for the future. You know where you are headed and what you want out of life. You have also developed a solid structure to manage your time, energy and effort to give you the freedom to bring your plans to life.

Of course, now you have all this figured out, everything will run smoothly. Well, not necessarily. For some of us there is a real risk in taking these first steps too seriously, a tendency towards perfectionism and becoming workaholics, driving ourselves into the ground. When we lose perspective and our plans start to run us, rather than the other way around, the life we want is always just out of reach.

To navigate our way through the natural lows and highs of life, we need tools to buoy our success, ways to maintain our energy, the right amount of stress, affirmations to keep us on track, a healthy dose of confidence and plenty of reasons to laugh. We also need opportunities to stretch ourselves forward with passion projects, travel plans and bucket lists. We need our own 'recipes for success' to guide us towards the lives we most want to live.

What's in your success toolkit?

As you begin to make your purpose, vision and hopes a reality by consistently following through on your plans, you'll find that even though you show up committed, confident and courageous, things won't always pan out the way you want.

To maintain your energy and enthusiasm, regardless of how your day is unfolding, create your own success toolkit to help you keep going. Think of this as your equipment for looking after yourself as your journey unfolds.

There are lots of different ways to relax and nurture yourself, so you need to identify the things that work for you. Think beyond soaking in a scented bath or booking in for a facial – your mind needs to be supported just as much as your body. Working out what keeps you functioning at your best is called self-care, and it's a vital part of your success toolkit.

Cheryl Richardson, author of *The Art of Extreme Self-Care,* sums it up perfectly: 'Extreme self-care involves surrounding myself with people who are smart, self-aware and only interested in two-way relationships. It means taking bold steps, such as eliminating clutter from my life, for good; creating a soul-nourishing work and home environment, and keeping it that way; getting my financial act together so that I always have choices about how to live my life; and not making any commitments whatsoever out of guilt and obligation.' ›

SOME IDEAS FOR YOUR TOOLKIT

Things you may want to include are:

➤ **Authenticity gut check**
   Are you being YOU? Are you walking the talk and living your values?

➤ **Gratitude moments**
   Are you expressing gratitude for your supporters?

➤ **Self-love makeover**
   Are you looking in the mirror daily and connecting with who you are? Try smiling at your own reflection.

➤ **Story audit**
   Are the stories you're telling yourself creating beliefs that pull you forward?

➤ **Sleep bank**
   Are you decompressing and refuelling at night? Remember, sleep is our best medicine.

➤ **Acts of kindness**
   Are you giving to others by performing kind acts? This can be one of the best ways to lower stress levels.

➤ **What's working well?**
   Are you building on your strengths to get the results you want?

➤ **Jolts of joy**
   Have you genuinely laughed today?

➤ **Grit goal**
   Are you persisting with things that are a little challenging, and celebrating your efforts?

---

* *There is no right or wrong answer by which you define success.*

Be on your own 'to do' list

What are you doing for YOU today? This is where you start making sure you're included on your own 'to do' list. To sustain your optimal level of wellbeing, you need to take responsibility for scheduling in self-care, and treat it as the most important job in the world. This does not mean booking a holiday or shopping trip, but rather a deep level of care. It is about honouring yourself and not succumbing to anxiety or guilt about looking after yourself.

Making pleasure a priority is critical for extreme self-care. Real pleasure is achieved by developing habits that make you feel happy and nurtured. These could include listening to the music you love on your commute to work, drinking your favourite tea each morning, buying flowers for your work desk, going out for dinner once a fortnight with friends, seeing a movie every month, taking a break from work in the middle of the day to get out into nature, booking a regular pedicure, visiting art galleries, organising regular walks with friends or curling up with a book on Sunday afternoons.

Your success toolkit is your immediate go-to when you are feeling a bit out of control, stressed and stuck. It is your personal back-up for when life throws a curve ball or you're just worn out, and will help put you back in the driver's seat again.

How do you maintain your energy?

It's completely within your power to manage your energy levels so they work for you. The human body has basic needs for energy production and maintenance, and addressing them will help you function at your peak. Habits are the key, so ensure your energy toolkit becomes part of your weekly and daily habits, just like brushing your teeth.

ENERGY TOOLKIT

- ➤ Sleep: it is both recovery and preparation. Make sure you're getting at least 7 hours a night. If you're having trouble getting to sleep, avoid looking at a backlit portable screen (laptop, smartphone, tablet) for at least an hour before bed. Also, keep your bedroom for the sole purpose of sleep (no screens allowed!).
- ➤ Water: hydrate throughout the day.
- ➤ Eating habits: 70 per cent of the way you feel is due to what you are eating.
- ➤ Stretch: extend your muscles each day.
- ➤ Move: get the blood flowing. Many people are starting to use standing desks, as sitting too much is now understood to be dangerous to our health. Standing and moving around regularly also helps you feel more alert.
- ➤ Mini-pauses: take 5-minute breaks throughout the day.
- ➤ Attitude: having a positive attitude gives you energy, while being negative drains you.
- ➤ Silence: grab it and cherish it.

TRY A 2-MINUTE MEDITATION

A growing body of research suggests we would all benefit from daily meditation. So how do we integrate it into our lives in a way that's achievable and still gives us the benefits we need?

I meditate in the morning and the evening, and have a collection of guided meditations that suit a range of needs for my mind and body. Outside this regular practice, I often sit in silence in the car for a few minutes before the school pick-up or when I'm in a queue or traffic jam. It's a small change, but it has had one of the biggest impacts on my physical health and my mindset.

Not sure you can pull it off? Try just 2 minutes a day. This is much easier and more sustainable than thinking you have to commit to a daily half-hour practice, and you are much more likely to keep at it. You don't need to rush out and buy a meditation cushion, join a class or even try to sit still for 15 minutes – not yet. Just start by being still for 2 minutes each day and noticing your breath. Breathe in and out through your nose, counting slowly to four for the intake and then four for the release. Controlled, calm breathing like this helps us relax, focus and let go of any stress we may be feeling. It also helps connect our minds to our bodies, which puts us back in the moment and is a powerful tool for mindfulness.

Do you have the right amount of stress?

Do you ever feel stressed out? The good news is that a little bit of stress isn't bad for us. It's our body's way of focusing our attention and energy on a particular problem or opportunity, and harnessing all our resources to solve it or move us forward.

But when stress accumulates, hour after hour, day after day, week after week, it starts to wreak havoc on our bodies, our minds and our relationships. We simply aren't built to handle large amounts of the hormones, such as cortisol and adrenaline, that stress generates. When stress overwhelms us or lingers for too long, it can leave us unable to make decisions, harm our ability to learn, damage our health and cause us to pull away from others.

60-SECOND STRESS BUSTERS

Here are some fast, tried and tested ways to reset your stress levels. Spend the time:

- ➤ Breathing deeply and slowly.
- ➤ Stretching.
- ➤ Drawing a picture.
- ➤ Sipping a glass of water.
- ➤ Walking.
- ➤ Counting with your eyes closed.
- ➤ Thinking about the bigger picture to gain perspective.
- ➤ Laughing.
- ➤ Sharing the problem with someone who is a good listener.

RESET YOURSELF

Feeling stressed? I have a list of things I run through to help me refocus and regain a sense of calmness. Try it yourself:

I LEARNT TODAY . . .

I'M GRATEFUL FOR . . .

I CAN LET GO OF . . .

I ACKNOWLEDGE MYSELF TODAY FOR . . .

I CAN RELEASE THE NEED TO BE . . .

I CHOOSE TO ENJOY TODAY BECAUSE . . .

I WANT TO FOCUS ON . . .

I BELIEVE IN MYSELF BECAUSE . . .

What are you affirming?

Your mindset has everything to do with success. Your personal beliefs determine the way you feel and act, and ultimately dictate where you'll put your energy. They shape your vision and hopes, and affirm what you think is possible when it comes to the kind of success you want to enjoy. If you say you can, you might pull it off. If you say you can't, you'll never get started.

The word 'affirmation' comes from the Latin *affirmare*, originally meaning 'to make steady, strengthen'. When we put into words what we want to be or what we want to happen, we are empowering ourselves and reassuring our minds about the possibilities. Affirmations help break the patterns of negative thoughts and move us towards more positive feelings and actions.

Psychologist Dr Carmen Harra has some excellent affirmations to get you started:

- I am the architect of my life; I build its foundation and choose its contents.
- Today, I am brimming with energy and overflowing with joy.
- My body is healthy; my mind is brilliant; my soul is tranquil.
- I am superior to negative thoughts and low actions.
- I have been given endless talents which I will begin to utilise today.
- I forgive those who have harmed me in my past and peacefully detach from them.
- A river of compassion washes away my anger and replaces it with love.

- ➤ (If you're married) My marriage is becoming stronger, deeper and more stable each day.
- ➤ I possess the qualities needed to be extremely successful.
- ➤ Happiness is a choice. I base my happiness on my own accomplishments and the blessings I've been given.
- ➤ My ability to conquer my challenges is limitless; my potential to succeed is infinite.
- ➤ (For those who are unemployed) I deserve to be employed and paid well for my time, efforts and ideas. Each day, I am closer to finding the perfect job for me.
- ➤ I am courageous and I stand up for myself.
- ➤ My thoughts are filled with positivity and my life is plentiful with prosperity.
- ➤ Today, I abandon my old habits and take up new, more positive ones.
- ➤ Many people look up to me and recognise my worth; I am admired.
- ➤ I am blessed with an incredible family and wonderful friends.
- ➤ I acknowledge my own self-worth; my confidence is soaring.
- ➤ Everything that is happening now is happening for my ultimate good.
- ➤ Today, I will let myself shine.

How can you maintain confidence?

How confident do you feel about your ability to create the life you want to be living? Researchers have found that believing we can improve our abilities is actually more important than believing in our abilities themselves. Confidence comes from believing that with the courage to learn, the willingness to make an effort and the persistence to keep practising, we're each born with the capacity to make continuous improvements in our lives.

When we have confidence in our ability to grow we fear failure less, we're not as attached to outcomes and negative feedback doesn't undo us. Think of Thomas Edison, who persisted through a thousand failed attempts at inventing the lightbulb before he succeeded; now that's confidence! You can build your confidence by:

➤ **Using your strengths regularly**
These are the things you do well and enjoy. Visit the VIA Institute on Character's website (www.viame.org) for a great tool to help you identify your strengths.

➤ **Surrounding yourself with people who love learning**
People who are on their own path of growth will be happy to share the journey.

➤ **Celebrating efforts, not just results**
Don't focus solely on outcomes; acknowledge the efforts you're making along the way.

➤ **Sharing your growth**
Tell your dream team the small wins and the big results.

➤ **Focusing on what's within your control**
Know you've made your best effort and let the rest go.

As an achievement junkie with a tendency towards perfectionism, one of the most effective (and totally unexpected) ways I've found to boost my confidence is to embrace my vulnerability. This means accepting who I am and leaving behind who I think I should be. It allows me to be imperfect and to be okay with this part of my journey, and it significantly increases the depth of my happiness, contentment and confidence. I might not be the best speaker, have the best book or cook the best meal for my family, but I'm here, I'm showing up, I'm willing to learn and I'm willing to accept that makes me good enough.

Author, researcher and scholar Brené Brown has spent a decade studying vulnerability, courage, worthiness and shame. She suggests vulnerability is the birthplace of innovation, creativity and change, and that it is our most accurate measurement of courage. It is the gateway to intimacy with ourselves and others. It is about having the confidence to be honest about our fears, how we're feeling and what we need, and to be willing to share this with others.

Setting boundaries is a great example. It's something that people don't think about as requiring vulnerability, but saying 'no' and protecting our time – whether it's family time, creative time or our self-care time – is a huge act of confidence in a culture that values productivity so highly.

BEING VULNERABLE

- ➤ Celebrate your imperfections.
- ➤ Recognise others who are being vulnerable and authentic.
- ➤ Be fully aware of how you feel in the moment.
- ➤ Own your emotions.
- ➤ Reveal something.

---

* *My mind is in charge of my confidence.*

Do you have enough reasons to laugh?

When did you last have a really good laugh? You know, one of those outbursts that literally shakes your whole body. When you can hardly breathe and your sides are hurting afterwards. If you can't remember the last time you really laughed, it's a clear sign you need to make room for a little more humour and playfulness in your life. Humour balances the seriousness of life, and it's what helps you endure challenges.

While it's great to celebrate achievements and accomplishments, it's just as important to enjoy the journey – and this is where laughter plays a huge role. It may not be a cure-all, but laughter is good for you on many levels.

- **Laughter relaxes your whole body**
  A good, hearty laugh relieves physical tension and stress, relaxing your muscles for up to 45 minutes afterwards.

- **Laughter triggers the release of endorphins**
  The body's natural feel-good chemicals, endorphins promote an overall sense of wellbeing.

- **Laughter boosts the immune system**
  It decreases stress hormones and increases your body's production of white blood cells and infection-fighting antibodies, thus improving your resistance to disease.

- **Laughter protects the heart**
  Laughter improves the function of blood vessels and increases blood flow, which can help protect against heart attack and other cardiovascular problems.

WAYS TO LAUGH MORE

You can find more reasons to laugh by:

- ➤ **Smiling**
  This is where laughter begins, so find reasons to smile and let it take over your body.

- ➤ **Spending time with fun, playful people**
  Seek out family and friends who make you laugh.

- ➤ **Moving towards laughter**
  When you hear people laughing, join them; laughter is highly contagious.

- ➤ **Joining a laughter club**
  These are groups that get together for the express purpose of laughing.

- ➤ **Watching comedy**
  This can be in any form you like – a YouTube clip, live act, television show or movie.

- ➤ **Reading funny books or comics**
  Start each day with a funny quote or cartoon.

What or who makes you laugh? Invest some recovery time in these activities and people.

✱ *The most important friendship you can have is with yourself.*

What are
your passion projects?

Is there something you do just for the love of it? Not necessarily to make money. Not necessarily for fame and accolades. But just because it indulges your deep desire to create. To bring your ideas to life, in whatever form they may take.

It could be a hobby, such as painting, gardening or playing an instrument. It could be a community project, such as coaching your kids' sports team, organising the annual street party or providing companionship at the local seniors' centre.

Passion projects and hobbies are vital for fostering growth and development. They ensure we don't end up regretting the things we wish we'd done, and they offer stress relief, lower your stress hormones, stave off burnout, provide pleasure and gratification, and keep life full of colour and vitality.

CHOOSE YOUR PASSIONS

Here are some examples to get you going, remembering that whatever you want to do, it needs to be built into your habit map or diaries to ensure you find the time to make it happen:

- Photography
- Gardening
- Reading
- Writing
- Cooking
- Movies
- Golf
- Swimming
- Playing an instrument
- Singing
- Sports
- Yoga
- Drawing and painting
- Dancing
- Knitting

What is your passion project? What can you see yourself doing for a long time so that you become passionate about it?

Do you travel with purpose?

Where do you long to visit? What amazing things would you like to do when you get there? Whenever you travel with purpose, more world abundance opens up to you, more relationships are created and, most importantly, you can incorporate some of your bucket list and hobbies into your trip.

Holidays can be incredible experiences when you travel to learn, meet new people and grow as a person. Trips with an intention, such as photography tours, art adventures, cooking classes and golf holidays, can be particularly rewarding, as can trips where you are giving back, such as going overseas to do volunteer work. These are some of the memories you savour in life, because you come home feeling inspired.

Get online and start a detailed investigation of the places you would like to visit. Look beyond the main tourist sites to find opportunities to get off the beaten track and put yourself in areas where you'll be more likely to meet the locals and experience their way of life. It's hard to truly understand a different culture when you're viewing it through the windows of a car or bus. Here are some questions to ask yourself when you're researching your next trip:

- ➤ What is my intention for this adventure?
- ➤ What could I learn as I go?
- ➤ How could I immerse myself in this culture?
- ➤ What opportunities does this offer me?
- ➤ What would make this trip memorable?

Have you become too comfortable?

If your life is starting to feel a little dull and boring, it's a sure sign your comfort zone needs stretching. When we take on new opportunities or challenges there's a natural learning curve that comes with mastering new ways of thinking, feeling and being. Over time, we get better at putting the pieces together to get the results we want, adapting to this new way of life and settling into a comfortable groove. This feeling of comfort is a place of peace and relief, but if we remain comfortable and unchallenged for too long we stagnate and become bored.

For me, travelling overseas on my own, taking on jobs I thought were too hard, and continually looking for ways to stretch myself have led to personal growth, increased life satisfaction and happiness. Things can go wrong, but having resilience, perspective and a good foundation of values to fall back on makes this process exciting.

Margie Warrell, a courage coach, asks these questions:

➤ Do I keep doing what's always been done or challenge old assumptions and try new approaches to problems?

➤ Do I proactively seek new challenges or just manage those I already have?

➤ Do I risk being exposed and vulnerable, or act to protect my pride and patch of power?

➤ Do I ask for what I really want or just for what I think others want to give me?

➤ Do I 'toot my horn' to ensure others know what I'm capable of or just hope my efforts will be noticed?

➤ Do I speak my mind or bite my lip, lest I ruffle feathers or subject myself to criticism?

Too often we let our mistakes and setbacks define us. But it's really our attitude towards failure that determines whether it's going to be an experience from which we can learn and grow, or one that stops us in our tracks. Each year, I set a monthly challenge that's a little out of my comfort zone so that I can foster my continual growth.

TEST YOUR COMFORT ZONE

➤ **Commit**
Get out of your comfort zone as often as possible.
If you don't challenge yourself and make yourself a little uncomfortable, you won't grow, evolve and flourish as a human being.

➤ **When you're ripe, you rot**
Make sure you're always a little bit 'green', as it means you're still trying new things and have the capacity to learn. And realise that there's always room for improvement.

➤ **Crawl, walk, run**
Don't force yourself to leap into the deep end immediately. Break down bigger goals into smaller chunks, and slowly take on more daring challenges.

➤ **Be curious**
Throw away your assumptions about what will happen and get curious instead.

➤ **Mix it up**
Experiment with activities you wouldn't normally do. Numbers geek? Try a course in meditation. IT guru? Enrol in cooking classes. Creative thinker? Sign up for martial arts. Open up new sides of yourself and explore them!

---

* *Invite the adventure of the new day ahead and look forward to the experiences it brings.*

What is on your bucket list?

What do you want to do before you die? Put simply, a bucket list is a list of things you really want to do before you die – a play on the phrase 'kick the bucket'.

What do your boldest dreams entail? These might be big dreams, such as travelling the world. They might be smaller ambitions, such as playing the guitar publicly. Whatever the size, you have to work towards them just as you work towards your goals, which is why it's important to write them down. By creating a bucket list, you turn your dreams into attainable, tangible goals that are within your reach.

Your bucket list is there to inspire, to represent your values, to put fire in your belly and to excite your brain. Whenever I read something that inspires and appeals to me, I write it on my bucket list so I always feel that I am moving forward. One of the ways I like to do this is by creating a twenty-year plan. It sounds daunting, but it is the simplest thing to do as it creates perspective instantly.

Think about it for a moment. Where will you be in twenty years' time? For example, if you're forty years old right now, where will you be when you're sixty? When an age is attached to the question, a vague picture of what your life might be like emerges because it gives an age to the people around you – your partner, your children, your parents and your friends. Suddenly, you can see what 'stage' of life you'll be at in twenty years' time, and that helps you start to picture what you want your life to look like at that point.

TIPS TO CREATE YOUR TWENTY-YEAR PLAN

➤ Start with a blank piece of paper or spreadsheet.

➤ Create four columns: Year, Career, Home and Family.

➤ Write in things you're fairly sure of: your age in twenty years' time, plus your partner's and kids' ages, your stage of life, your health and your career. Once this solid, knowable information is plugged in, it makes it easier to open your mind up to dream big.

➤ List every holiday you dream of taking and every hobby you want to develop. Look at your twenty-year plan and work out where your milestone birthdays and anniversaries will fall. Start thinking about the celebrations you'd like to create, and dates when you may be able to match up your dream holiday destinations with major milestones.

➤ Add other things from your bucket list and when you'd like to make them happen.

➤ Think about education – are there courses or further study you or your partner would like to undertake? If you have children, think about where you would like them to attend school, both primary and secondary.

➤ Consider your living arrangements, too. Are you already in your dream home or would you like to renovate or move house? Are you happy with where you live or do you hope to move to another area further down the track? Will you need to upsize or downsize at some point?

YOUR BUCKET LIST

Think about the following areas and what you'd like to achieve in each:

Career	*Adventure*
Recreation	*Fitness*
Knowledge	*Spiritual*
Activities	*Investments*
Travel	*Education*
Family	*Personal growth*
Home	*Fun*
Friends	*Service*

WHAT IS YOUR RECIPE FOR SUCCESS?

Everyone has their own definition of success, and these can vary considerably. Rather than relying on a one-size-fits-all definition, it's important to devise your own recipe for success to guide you through life. It needs to be something you'll see often, so that it becomes a part of who you are and can influence your decisions on a daily basis. I recommend programming it into your weekly plan. When I ask my clients to create their recipe for success, I suggest they use the word SUCCESS as an acronym:

- ➤ **S:** Sort out your values.
- ➤ **U:** Understand your beliefs and behaviours.
- ➤ **C:** Choose your vision for yourself.
- ➤ **C:** Construct hopes to support your vision and brand.
- ➤ **E:** Evaluate and acknowledge each step of your journey and progress.
- ➤ **S:** Simplify and structure your processes.
- ➤ **S:** Smile and enjoy your ideal setup for optimal living and success.

---

* *Success means freedom of choice in my daily life.*

* *Success means living a purposeful life.*

SUMMARY

—

Taking the time to develop a higher level of self-awareness around these different success factors has made decisions in my life so much easier, and my health and wellbeing so much stronger. I've achieved more within my career because of the foundations I have built. When I lost my health to chronic fatigue syndrome I determined I would never go back there, so my success recipe and toolkit are essentials, ensuring I'm taking care of myself while living the life I choose.

As your plans begin to pay off and you begin to tick off your successes, you need to have the tools to maintain the life you're creating. Drawing on your success toolkit, maintaining your energy, ensuring you have the right amount of stress, plenty of reasons to laugh, affirmations to move you forward and enough confidence to keep pulling it all off will help you navigate the inevitable highs and lows we all experience. Along the way, keep stretching beyond your comfort zone by making time for your passion projects, creating your twenty-year bucket list and staying true to your own recipe for success.

TIPS AND TRICKS

—

- ➤ Embed your energy toolkit into your weekly habits and daily actions – make time for self-care.

- ➤ Collect and store the affirmations that work for you.

- ➤ Start a gratitude jar, journal or photo book.

- ➤ Try to meditate for 2 minutes each day.

- ➤ In the shower, check on your breathing. Before you go to sleep, make sure you are breathing correctly.

- ➤ Make your passwords something you want to be or are aiming for so that you are typing a daily affirmation when you enter them.

- ➤ Start a bucket list book, or twenty-year plan.

- ➤ Write on your bathroom mirror whatever you need in order to maintain confidence for the day or week.

- ➤ Practise being vulnerable with others about how you're feeling and asking for what you need.

- ➤ Stress busters can be booked in. My phone is constantly reminding me to breathe.

- ➤ Schedule time for your hobbies.

- ➤ When trying new things, have the 'courage to be uncomfortable'.

- ➤ Book a trip with purpose and intention.

- ➤ Prepare food for tomorrow and fill your water bottle each weeknight.

- ➤ Create your 'to do' list for the next day the night before.

- ➤ Make a rule of no phones when eating.

Plant the seeds for success and nurture them, and you will be rewarded with a life that blooms.

SABBATICAL

—

Taking a pause is exciting, invigorating, life changing and possible. Taking time out to see life from a different perspective or country can give us the energy and creativity to live life optimally.

SABBATICAL

—

Taking a 'pause' in life was something I had heard of, but didn't think was possible. You can only do it when you are young and responsibility-free, right? When I was twenty-one years old, I travelled the world with a backpack for two years and I think that was the probably the time I learnt the most in life – a sense of freedom that came hand-in-hand with fear, excitement, opportunity, fun, loneliness, self-acceptance and incredible experiences, both good and bad, which I have always treasured.

New York graphic designer and TED speaker Stefan Sagmeister takes a year off every seven years, saying he will retire five years later to balance it all out. Listen to his talk (www.ted.com/talks/stefan_sagmeister_the_power_of_time_off) and you will see that, with the right planning, a sabbatical can be one of the smartest career moves you can make. Why wait until retirement; why not have these incredible experiences along the way to gain clarity and energy? Taking these breaks when we are fit enough to challenge ourselves, do what we want and experience the world in new ways really makes sense.

Before you say a sabbatical is not for you, let's debunk a few myths.

MYTH	REALITY
I cannot afford it professionally.	You really won't miss much while you're away.
It's unaffordable financially.	It is approximately half a year's salary – spread over a lifetime it's not that much.
We can't take the kids out of school.	I would argue that our children learned more on our trip – science, geography, physical education, biology, English, cultural studies, history, anthropology, mechanics, engineering, art, photography, psychology, humanities, popular culture, community life, economics, life skills, orienteering, positive role modelling, you name it!
If I can't afford to travel overseas, is there any point?	There are plenty of amazing experiences to be had on our own doorstep. You might like to visit the outback; explore a state you haven't visited before; do a house swap in another city; stay on a working farm and experience shearing and mustering; go camping or caravaning; live on an island; rent a beachhouse; explore the rainforest; or take part in an environmental and wildlife conservation project.
I need to wait until retirement.	Life is unpredictable – you don't know what your health will be like or how long you'll live.
Successful people don't have time for sabbaticals.	Successful people take sabbaticals to gain clarity, energy and motivation.
It is impossible to plan.	You'll make it happen if you want to; just book it and everything else will fall into place.
It is just a holiday and won't change my work/life in any way.	It is a major life experience; you'll learn, evolve, grow and develop your human self. It is a chance to reboot!
When I get back, my career will be on the rocks.	You'll be able to offer more to your career if you are not resentful of it.

Mapping out a plan

When our children were born, my husband and I went through our twenty-year plan, basically covering when our children would start school, when they would start secondary school and when they would finish. We asked ourselves a few simple questions: When would we like to take a 'pause' in life? When would it be possible? What ages would work best for us? What would be the optimal time for our children to travel and experience the world with us? What would we regret not doing? How could we make it happen?

We pencilled in two years where we thought it would be possible, when our kids wouldn't need to do homework and could just be kids. We also had other criteria – our son and daughter had to be old enough to bike, walk and experience the world. We named our sabbatical 'The Pause' and we called all the steps required to get there 'Operation Too Easy'. I have to say that it is the best thing I have done in my life: a beautiful, incredibly special and inspiring trip that I will treasure forever. Of course, I am already planning the next one.

A SABBATICAL OR A CAREER BREAK?

What is the difference between the two? Well, a sabbatical is when you take your time out and return to your job with the blessing of your employer. It is a time where many employers assist employees to take a business course, do volunteer work or travel. (I know of an enlightened company that supported a senior employee to do yoga teacher training.) The idea is always to return to the company and continue with the organisation that has supported the sabbatical. In Australia, long service leave is the vehicle for many people to take a sabbatical without losing their income stream.

A career break is when you resign and consciously take a break. Many people do this before setting up their own business. They take time to breathe, plan, learn languages, write that script they've always wanted to, spend some time at home with their family or simply take stock of life. Many people take one before changing their career path.

QUESTIONS TO HELP YOU GAIN CLARITY

- ➤ Do I want a break?
- ➤ Do I need time to rest, recharge, recommit?
- ➤ What would make my working life shine?
- ➤ What do I want to learn?
- ➤ How much will it cost?
- ➤ Will my current employer be open to it?
- ➤ Will my business suffer?
- ➤ What will it do for my health?
- ➤ Where do I dream of going?
- ➤ Who else has done this and what was their experience?

---

*   *The only way to take a break in life, or press the 'pause' button, is to make the decision that you want to take it.*

How do you take a break in life?

Taking a break is part of your plan if you want it to be. Remember that you know your values, your vision, your goals, your structures and your passion projects or hobbies. And in the same way that our cars need refuelling, our technical tools need recharging and our soil needs fertilising, our minds need space to be able to think and our bodies need to move, stretch and breathe to be able to function optimally.

To press the 'pause' button, the first step is to make the decision that you want to do this. Make the decision and tell someone. When we decided, we wrote it down in our planner and looked at it. It looked great, but then our emotions ran crazy. Can we really do that? What would people think? What would happen to our jobs? How could we afford it? Wow, how bold would we be if we did that? This turned quite quickly into: we can do it! Wouldn't it be great; how adventurous and how glorious would it be to have freedom and a blank slate each day? Imagine seeing the world through the eyes of our children; imagine leaving the phone behind.

---

* *A pause can provide gifts and abundance that money can't buy.*
* *I left my phone in Melbourne and got on the plane. I did not make a phone call for twenty weeks. And I lived!*

Our big pause – five months

WHERE: United States, British Virgin Islands, Mexico

WHEN: 2013

WHO: Me and my husband, our two children, and a visiting aunty and grandparent along the way

HOW LONG: Twenty weeks

ESSENTIALS: A great attitude, courage, fear, a plan and my camera

CONTRABAND ITEMS: Smartphone, watch, make-up, clients, high heels, suits and fancy clothes

GOAL: To explore, to connect, to bond, to experience, to learn, to secure meaning and to recharge body and mind

THE OUTCOME: Freedom, energy, fun, adventures of a lifetime, new skills, stories and a feeling of great abundance in life. A sense that we are in charge of our own destiny, so keep planning for greatness and depth in life. Oh, and we all liked each other!

When we decided to take our pause, it was important that we had clarity on the purpose. I wanted to recharge my body and mind. I wanted to have the time to learn photography and capture the moments that would help me be mindful, present and enjoy the moment. My husband, Michael, had been a CEO for ten years and was really in need of a break and recharge. Our ten years of marriage had been incredible so far, with two booming careers, the births of two children who were now in school, marathons run, house renovated and full commitment to being who we wanted to be. It was time to take a breath, to enjoy, to savour, to celebrate, to stop.

OUR PLAN

➤ **Altitude living**
Eight weeks in Colorado, at 2103 metres above sea level in Steamboat Springs. Hiking, biking, fishing, reading, photography, yoga, exercise, breathing, decompressing from the world.

➤ **The Road Bear RV**
Six weeks on the road, covering 6000 kilometres across Utah, Colorado, Nevada and California, experiencing people, cities, nature, animals and roadhouses, taking photographs and renewing our wedding vows in Las Vegas.

➤ **A change of season**
Back to Colorado for three weeks to see the leaves begin to turn in autumn, visit the rodeos, ride horses and recalibrate our bodies and minds, do yoga, read and see the first snowfall of the season.

➤ **A Caribbean calypso**
Two weeks in the British Virgin Islands in the Caribbean. Charter and drive our own boat. Swim, snorkel, live on the boat, meet people and experience ocean, sand, navigation, photography, fishing, heat and the Caribbean way of life.

➤ **Signing off from Cancun**
One week in Cancun, Mexico. Rest and prepare to re-enter our lives of career, work, school, family, activities, learning, sports and so on.

---

* *A 'pause' is taking time to breathe, to enjoy, to savour, to celebrate, to stop.*

Enjoying the great, and incredibly beautiful, outdoors in Colorado; hitting the road in the RV, with bike riding, buffalo sightings, and cool dips in tranquil lakes; renewing our vows in Vegas.

Blissful boating and beaching in the Caribbean and Cancun. Completely rested, reinvigorated and recharged, we are ready to return to life back home.

A peek in our writing journals

Before you begin your sabbatical, or 'pause', is a great time to journal, as it's a useful way to explore your thoughts, fears and expectations about the changes ahead.

{ Shannah }

There are so many emotions now that I have stopped working. I am an achievement junkie, so it is exciting to have the opportunity to think about achievement in new ways. I am excited to experience new things and, being a beach person, to see what it is like to be a mountain person. I am excited to have time; time to explore, feel, learn, grow, be in the moment and master more of myself, work on being the best version of me I can be in life. And I'm excited to get out of Melbourne in winter; I really struggle with the cold.

I'm also feeling fear about leaving my beloved routines and structures, and anxiety that I may not actually like being in a pause. That sounds quite bizarre, but I love my job, my home, my existence here in Melbourne. The 'what ifs?' are there in my mind. What if I don't like it? What if I don't get the space I need as a person who likes calm in her life? What if I don't like being with the kids round the clock? I have to challenge myself to have no expectations of the family or the places, and to enjoy everything for what it is.

I am filled with determination to learn. To learn more about photography, about life, about computers and IT, as I am falling behind. Michael is our IT department and I have let him be that, but I need to learn how it all works so I can help myself. I want to think about the next stage of our lives and what I need to do to capture and enjoy every moment. ›

I am feeling gratitude, bucketloads of it. Firstly, that we are fortunate enough to be able to do this trip. I am grateful that Michael and I are both adventurous and courageous enough to make the bold decisions and make things happen for ourselves. Neither of us wait for opportunities, we both go out and make them. I am grateful I have the courage to leave my business for a while and let it breathe, to be authentic and live the life I have chosen. I have incredible gratitude for my marriage, and that we operate as a team; that we have had the best ten years and that each year seems to get better, faster and more exciting than the last.

But mostly, I am deeply happy. With my life, with my marriage, with my beautiful children. We are all healthy, physically and mentally. And this is why I want to take a pause – to deeply experience this.

{ Michael }

Well, here I am. Sitting in Dubai, after a work trip, about to jump on a plane and spend 14 hours flying home before packing up and heading off on another 30-hour journey in six days' time. Normally, this would be something to dread, however this time I can't wait to jump into row 59 with my family and begin a trip we'll remember for the rest of our lives.

I've always had a strong motivation to take time out and spend five months overseas as a family unit. Firstly, because of my vivid, fond childhood memories of an extended road trip with my family, and secondly, because I believe we owe it to ourselves to stop, think and work out how the hell we got to where we are today and how we can continue to make our lives awesome in the future.

I am proud we take risks. I am proud we act, rather than talk, and I am most proud that we have done it all by ourselves with no help from anyone. There is little doubt life will throw curve balls at us from time to time, but this trip will be a bonding experience that will be ours and ours alone.

I think the reason I have managed to be successful in my job and my life over the past ten years is mostly due to Shannah – how amazing she is at home, in business and in life. She sets standards that don't allow me to drop my guard or accept the easy path. It has become second nature for me to take chances and follow my instincts.

I love my kids. I love spending quality time with them. I hope to find a new level of connection and calm in our relationship. I look forward to bonding with them both. We are a close family, but there is more work to do there.

I can't wait to go home to the mountains. In some funny way I know they have been a big part of my life. I love the casualness and informality – mountain people don't take themselves too seriously, but they really appreciate and love the environment around them.

I'm looking forward to learning new skills. It has been a long time since I actually started something from scratch, as a beginner. Whether it is biking, fishing or RV-ing, I am looking forward to learning again.

So let's embrace the pause, open our minds, get on that plane and get the hell out of Hampton for a while! Bring it on.

Reading these pre-departure journals again after our trip really heightened what we got out of it. We had a greater appreciation for the bold steps we had taken to make sure that what we wanted most in life actually happened, and I realised that my fears about being away for so long were unfounded.

Writing journals before and after holidays or before a big deal is made, or even just writing down thoughts and emotions, can be really helpful in aiding our growth and evolution. The more we understand ourselves and take ownership of our lives, the richer they will be.

SUMMARY

—

Only you can dictate the path of your life and orchestrate what you want to happen. You have to make those decisions and have the courage to take an informed risk to make your dreams come true.

Our 'pause' strengthened our marriage and our bonds as a family, and gave us gifts that went beyond the financial cost – experiences I will treasure for the rest of my life. It did cost money, but we saved, budgeted and took the risk to have a go, and it delivered.

{ What would your pause look like? }

Here is how you can start planning:

➤ Identify why you want a pause.
➤ How much time do you want? What would the start and end date be?
➤ Do you want land, sea, mountains, oceans, lakes?
➤ What will be different from where you are now?
➤ What is on your bucket list or in your dreams that you can incorporate?
➤ How would you finance your sabbatical?
➤ How would your structure your time?
➤ How would you re-enter the workforce?
➤ What is the purpose; what do you want to learn from this valuable time? ›

{ Some lessons learnt }

- ➤ Five months is not a long time.
- ➤ You need to have a basic plan, but make sure you leave space for spontaneity.
- ➤ Your attitude needs to be in the right place.
- ➤ You don't need much in life.
- ➤ If you want to live your dream, you need to book it and make it happen.
- ➤ You need an intention for your time out.
- ➤ Taking a break from your busy life is an exceptional way to connect and strengthen family bonds.
- ➤ Experiences are educational; your children will learn important life skills.
- ➤ Disconnecting is a great way to recharge.
- ➤ It's *your* break, so do your research and make sure it ticks as many of your boxes as possible (rather than the well-meaning suggestions of others!).
- ➤ Be realistic. Plan a break that is achievable and that you know you can budget for.

---

* *Remember, no matter how long you take, nothing significant will have changed when you get back; only you will have grown, evolved and experienced.*

TIPS AND TRICKS

—

- Do you want mini-breaks in your life or do you want to wait until retirement to have one big break?

- Plan with intention.

- Tell people your plans; this may open doors through friends of friends wherever you're going and it will also help firm up your commitment.

- You may like to consider a house swap.

- Write down where you want to go and what you want to achieve.

- Draw up a timeline of your life and plot where you want the breaks to be.

- Factor in some down time, particularly at the end of the break. A mixture of action, adventure, rest and relaxation is ideal.

- Search the internet for interesting things that happen around the time of your break. Cultural festivals, animal migrations, natural phenomena (such as the Northern Lights) and landscapes that are particularly beautiful in certain seasons (snow-capped mountains or mass flowerings) can all add to a break immeasurably.

- A slow pace gives us time to meet people, absorb a culture and experience daily life in different surrounds. Not to mention time to rest! Try not to race from one sight to the next.

- Encourage all your family to keep a journal.

SHINE

—

Find ecstasy in life; the mere sense of living is joy enough.

—

Emily Dickinson

SHINE

—

For me, this is the fun part when helping people create the lives they most want to be living. You see, after a while you might find that while everything is going along nicely, suddenly you want to quit, you feel bored or you start sabotaging yourself in a whole new way.

Why do we do this to ourselves? We're hardwired with a tremendous capacity to adapt to nearly all the good and bad things that happen in our lives. Whether it's a new relationship, a new job, improved health or newfound wealth, over time the shine starts to wear off and these hard-won changes in our lives start to deliver fewer and fewer rewards.

Unfortunately, while the thrill of victory and the agony of defeat have been found to abate over time, it appears we adapt much faster to the things we most enjoy. In fact, scientists believe we're prone to eventually take for granted pretty much every good thing that happens to us. It's why our energy, wellbeing and happiness often seem like they don't last. ›

If you feel you're starting to stagnate a little – physically, mentally, emotionally or spiritually – despite all the wonderful changes you've been making, it's important to know you're simply adapting and that this is a completely normal part of human functioning. To see how you're doing, quickly check in with these questions:

- ➤ How do you feel now?
- ➤ How is your confidence tracking?
- ➤ Where is your integrity sitting?
- ➤ Are your thoughts clear, strong and energetic?
- ➤ Have you fully embraced the fact that you are in the driver's seat?
- ➤ Do you rise and shine?
- ➤ Are you practising patience and mindfulness?
- ➤ Do your habits serve you well?
- ➤ Do your body, mind and soul feel healthy?
- ➤ Are you grateful for what's unfolding?

If you're not consistently flourishing, in this chapter you'll discover how you can prevent, slow down and even ward off stagnation altogether by paying more attention to what's happening, keeping life varied and dynamic, savouring and appreciating the changes, surprising yourself, making your activities more novel and staying with your purpose.

Are you staying on track?

Is your life running you or are you running it? With so much going on all the time, it's easy for life to slip away, despite our best intentions. To help stay on track, I start each day with this question: what is the purpose of today?

I find it easiest to answer this question by journalling. It's a private window to my soul that allows me to constantly check in with how things are really going. Journalling is for you and only you. It is the business of You. It is how you personally transform, grow and adapt as you consciously work on living a life you love. When we write, we gain true clarity on where we are at the moment and where we want to be growing. Where do we need to change and adapt to evolve?

When we write for ourselves we don't need to edit or spell check, we just let it all flow. We can pour what is in our minds onto paper and during that process we learn, question, grow and take ownership. This process can transform your life. Be honest with yourself, avoid self-criticism and editing, and don't hold yourself back.

Choose whatever form of journal works best for you: a notebook, diary, computer file or scrapbook; hard or soft cover; lined or unlined; colourful or black and white; free-form or structured.

THINGS TO INCLUDE

Words, drawings, pictures, photos, quotes, lists, websites and more, but most of all, yourself and your own precious thoughts. By writing down your thoughts, ideas and feelings, you are hard-wiring yourself for optimal living.

THOUGHT STARTERS

If you're new to journalling, fill in the chart below and use it as a guide to get your thoughts flowing.

FEELINGS

GOALS

DREAMS

RESPONSIBILITIES

ACHIEVEMENTS

RELATIONSHIPS

HEALTH (MENTAL AND PHYSICAL)

What are you focusing on?

Where attention goes, energy flows. By this stage you know more about yourself than you did when you started this process. You know how to structure your purpose and values into your days through your carefully designed planner, which takes into account every aspect of your life. But this journey isn't just about organisation. The real purpose of harnessing these strategies is so you can stop fretting about 'getting everything done' and instead relax in the knowledge that everything has been allocated its own time and space, allowing you to be fully present and enjoy each moment.

Wherever you are – at home, on a plane, in a meeting – if you are fully present, you can live life with depth, clarity and a sense of total abundance. Mindfulness brings calm and self-awareness, so you can make well-informed decisions each hour of the day. It can be practised all day, every day.

I like to use the five senses (sight, sound, taste, smell, touch) to guide my mindfulness practice. By engaging my senses, I can take control and find calm, even in the most stressful situations. Consider how a particular smell can trigger a happy memory. Perhaps it's the scent of roses taking you back to afternoon tea at your grandmother's house. The smells wafting out of a bakery may remind you of cooking with the kids (and lots of flour explosions, spoon licking and giggles). It is incredibly powerful to tap into these types of golden moments on a daily basis, simply by being mindful enough to engage your senses. ›

THE FIVE SENSES

- ➤ **Sight**
  Look, acknowledge, see. Notice the view, the formation of clouds, the brilliant colours that are abundant in nature.

- ➤ **Sound**
  Listen with closed eyes to what is happening around you. Also, listen to silence: it is powerful and re-energising, and you can hear yourself breathing. When you need to block out distracting sounds, try white noise or the sound of rain apps.

- ➤ **Smell**
  Your sense of smell can change your hormone levels and promote calm. Soap with essential oils, just-baked bread, freshly ground coffee – all of these scents can alter your state of mind and reduce your stress levels. Likewise, synthetic perfumes can often make you feel ill or stressed out, so avoid these where possible.

- ➤ **Taste**
  Be present for all your meals and savour every mouthful and how it makes you feel, such as the clean taste of a crisp apple or a hot coffee reaching your belly.

- ➤ **Touch**
  When you acknowledge the different textures around us – skin, a soft blanket, a sandy beach and so on – and think about how they make you feel, you can slow down time.

---

* *Mindfulness brings calm and a greater level of self-awareness, helping you make well-informed decisions each hour of the day.*

SENSORY EXPERIENCES YOU ENJOY

If we train ourselves to become more aware of the ordinary, life can quickly become extraordinary. Mindful eating, mindful walking, mindful talking, mindful living make life amazing! Jot down the things you enjoy from a sensory perspective:

TASTE *e.g. Salted caramels.*

TOUCH *e.g. Patting your pet.*

SOUND *e.g. Rain on a tin roof.*

SMELL *e.g. Freshly cut grass.*

SIGHT *e.g. Admiring local architecture.*

Do you need
to spice things up?

Feeling a little bored and seeing greyness in every direction of your life? This is a sure sign it's time to spice things up.

Our brains love novelty, so when we have adapted to our wellbeing practices, even the most tested approaches can stop bringing us much joy. But don't throw the baby out with the bathwater. Instead, think about what you can do to mix things up, do things a little differently or even just give them a rest for a while and then come back to them a few weeks later.

The tiniest changes make us feel refreshed and renewed; they don't have to be big and too hard – even a new coffee cup can make us feel great! Try some of these approaches to spice things up:

- ➤ Create a treasure box of all your favourite golden moments using photos, letters, mementos and the like.
- ➤ Commit to an exercise you've never tried before.
- ➤ Make a list of ten new places to visit.
- ➤ Update your music collection.
- ➤ Watch three classic movies.
- ➤ Explore a new restaurant each month.
- ➤ Reconnect with old friends you haven't seen for ages.
- ➤ Take a hike somewhere you've never been before.
- ➤ Rearrange your desk, furniture and cupboards, and declutter a little bit more; out with the old, in with the new.
- ➤ Set yourself mini-challenges for mindfulness.
- ➤ Be a tourist in your own town.
- ➤ Check your clothing suits the person you are; is it tired and old, does it make you feel confident? Get a bold piece going.

Remember, adaptation is just a normal part of life, so if you're feeling a little bored it's your brain's way of telling you to mix it up.

HOW YOU'RE GOING TO SPICE UP YOUR LIFE . . .

➤

➤

➤

➤

➤

➤

➤

➤

➤

➤

Are you having fun?

People often ask me, 'If you are so organised and committed, where's the fun?' The fun is in every day! The fun is in my attitude and not taking myself too seriously. Being organised lets me be spontaneous without sacrificing all the great work I'm doing.

Unfortunately, as we grow up, too many of us stop playing. 'Don't be childish.' 'Stop wasting time.' 'Quit mucking around.' Most of us hear these criticisms as we start to move away from childhood and the result is that by the time we've become adults, we've forgotten the growth and joy that playing brings to our lives. But the truth is, we are built to play and built through play. It is what makes us feel truly alive. Giving yourself permission to embrace a sense of spontaneity and fun can restore a healthy sense of play in the life you're living.

Play time can involve anything from simply being silly to playing sport, spending time doing something you love or just catching up with friends and having fun. The aim is to have a laugh, relax and, most importantly, let go and enjoy yourself. It can't be forced and you won't enjoy it if you're not feeling comfortable, so do whatever works for you (pranks and acting up might be right up one person's alley, but leave someone else feeling foolish). It may seem a little strange at first, especially if you haven't allowed play into your life for a long time, but soon you'll be right back in the swing of things.

I find that I need a weekly dose of fun, so I make it happen as often as I can to help me stay connected to the simple joys of life and the magic that comes from playing.

WAYS TO START PLAYING

- ➤ Memorise a few good jokes.
- ➤ Start a hobby just for the fun of it.
- ➤ Have a virtual vacation – 'go to Italy' for the day with some friends by eating Italian food, drinking Italian wine and seeing an Italian movie, for example.
- ➤ Ride a scooter and bring out your inner child.
- ➤ When running the bath for the kids, jump in yourself.
- ➤ Turn the music up and get your groove going.
- ➤ Start a girls'/boys' night out.
- ➤ Change your look.
- ➤ Book a 'mystery' flight.
- ➤ Roll down a hill.
- ➤ Gaze at the clouds and find shapes within them.
- ➤ Go to a big sporting event and cheer your heart out.
- ➤ Have a white Christmas.
- ➤ Listen to a seashell.
- ➤ Play golf with your friends.
- ➤ Make a photo album of your funniest pictures and photos.
- ➤ Go on a flying fox and get some thrills.
- ➤ Gallop down a hallway as though you are riding a horse.
- ➤ Start a regular family games night with your board games and cards.
- ➤ Go and see a musical or comedy show.
- ➤ Go away for the weekend on a last-minute deal.
- ➤ Build the biggest and best sandcastle on the beach.
- ➤ Play a prank on your partner or kids.
- ➤ Call a friend and just go out and have fun.

How do you savour and celebrate?

Have you ever been so focused on success you had no time to celebrate what you were achieving? I know it sounds crazy, but many of us are so busy striving to reach our goals we forget to make time to truly savour and appreciate the incredible outcomes we're creating. Yet people who revel in their successes are far more likely to enjoy them. It also helps to program your brain for more success to come.

WAYS YOU CAN SAVOUR AND CELEBRATE SUCCESS

- ➤ Share it with others.
- ➤ Throw a dinner party to celebrate.
- ➤ Take a mental picture of the moment and how you're feeling.
- ➤ Create a memento to remember what you've achieved.
- ➤ Shout for joy.
- ➤ Immerse yourself in the feeling of success.
- ➤ Indulge in your own victory dance.
- ➤ Hug someone.
- ➤ Forgive someone.
- ➤ Share your news.
- ➤ Tick things off.
- ➤ Reward yourself.

✱ *Your attitude is your altitude. It is how high you want to fly and how good you want your day to be.*

What are you appreciating?

When was the last time your heart overflowed with gratitude for everything you have? It might have been when you got your dream job, when your child got an award at school or when you achieved a lifelong goal. As we adapt to the good things in our lives, we can become blind to all we have to be thankful for: a warm bed on a cold night, a delicious meal with people we love, or clean air from the abundance of nature around us.

One of the simplest and most effective ways to ensure we don't take these things for granted is to practise gratitude, to extract the maximum joy and satisfaction from life. Gratitude helps prevent our expectations from becoming an unrealistic burden and keeps our tendency to compare ourselves with others in check. Practise it by counting your blessings each night, keeping a gratitude journal or writing a gratitude note each day and keeping them in a jar.

THINGS YOU MIGHT BE GRATEFUL FOR

- ➤ The hard things in life that have taught you lessons.
- ➤ Those who are serving you, such as your local barista.
- ➤ Technology – all the information it gives you and the ways in which it makes your life easier.
- ➤ Transport – everything that gets you from A to B.
- ➤ The food you eat.
- ➤ Your body, your mind and your soul.
- ➤ A good night's rest.

---

* *If we train ourselves to become more aware of the ordinary, life can very quickly become extraordinary.*

What are you hanging on to?

They say your attitude is your altitude. It determines how high you want to fly and how good you want your day to be. A poor attitude is like a flat tyre: if you don't change it, you won't go anywhere. Attitudes are developed by the experiences we encounter in our lives. Once you understand them, you can choose your attitude towards your life and your day. Are you choosing self-motivation and self-encouragement, or self-pity and hardship?

HOW IS YOUR ATTITUDE LOOKING?

➤ Are your words and thoughts positive or negative?

➤ Do you tend to say, 'It's too hard' or 'I'll have a go'?

➤ Are you open to financial prosperity?

➤ Are you acknowledging abundance?

➤ Is your intention of the day – your affirmation – charged with energy and faith?

➤ Are you saying, 'I am so busy, tired and stressed' or 'I am great'?

➤ What can you do right now to put yourself in motion, rather than staying stagnant?

➤ What attitude does your role model have? How can you move towards this right now?

➤ Do you believe you can change, and that a change in attitude could have the greatest impact?

➤ What is your attitude towards time?

One of the most important parts of this process is to be able to monitor your attitude and the effect it is having on your relationships, career and wellbeing. Your attitude affects everyone around you.

Are you being true to your purpose?

Staying true to your purpose – your north star – is the best way to keep your life from fading to greyness. Every few months I ask myself the following questions and write down the answers to ensure I remain in the driver's seat of life.

MY TOP 16 QUESTIONS

1   What risk would you take if you knew you could not fail? Where is fear holding you back?
2   What are the top five things you treasure in life?
3   If you didn't know your age, how old would you say you are?
4   Where is the line where you stop calculating risk and rewards, and just do it?
5   How aware are you of the positive or negative energy you are broadcasting?
6   At what time in your recent past have you felt most passionate, alive and well?
7   How are you manifesting opportunity in your life?
8   What are you avoiding?
9   Are you the author of your thoughts?
10 Are you listening to what you are actually saying?
11 What is the one job/cause/activity that could get you out of bed happily for the rest of your life? Are you doing it now?
12 What are you committed to?
13 What is your mindfulness practice doing for you?
14 Have you been the kind of friend you'd want to have?
15 What permission do you need/want to move forward?
16 We're always making choices. Are you choosing your story or is someone else?

SUMMARY

—

When things are going well, don't wait until you fall in a rut, get bored or give up to make changes. Every few months, take an hour to pay attention to how you're tracking, to spice things up and stay playful, to savour and celebrate your success, to feel grateful for all you have and to stay true to your purpose.

Allowing yourself to shine each and every day, as well as honouring yourself for doing so, is a principle worth taking on board. The finishing touches are the finest, smallest details that make the dedication and commitment all worth it. They honour your risks, courage, visions and attitudes, and let the changes you've created move naturally with the tides of life.

Many people report regrets at the end of their life, such as 'I wish I had let myself be happier,' 'I wish I hadn't worked so hard and so much' and 'I wish I'd had the courage to live true to myself and not the life others expected of me.' Don't let this be you. Taking control and getting into the driver's seat with these easy, small, snippets of focus ensure you are always being true to yourself and honouring who you are because you chose to do the work.

TIPS AND TRICKS

—

- Book a date in your diary every few months to check how you're tracking in life.

- Buy a journal you love to write in and every morning, ask: What's the purpose of today?

- Use all five senses, and be mindful of each sense.

- Be aware of, and appreciate, the ordinary.

- Sing more, hug more, live more.

- Celebrate your successes.

- Start a gratitude jar.

- Spice up your habits.

- Choose an attitude of altitude each day.

- Play, play, play!

- Stay true to your purpose.

- Allow yourself to shine each day.

It's often said that life is
a juggling act: family, health,
friendships, career . . .
The thing to remember is
that the career ball is the
one that bounces best
when it's dropped.

ONE LAST THING

—

We all want to be happy. We all want to strive for more. We all want to maximise the personal, professional and financial potential that life has to offer, but we'd prefer to do so without the stress, exhaustion and anxiety that is often bundled up with 'success'.

Many of us are over-achievers, so we're usually over-stimulated, with epic 'to do' lists, over-connectedness, competing priorities and crowded social calendars and social media pages.

As much as we want to flourish and succeed, sometimes we will fall off that path. That's okay. This book will bring you back to the basics and remind you of your vision and goals. It's as simple as that. Always come back and check in with your foundations.

And that is the purpose of this book. By understanding the strategies outlined in these pages, you can develop your own personal strategy for living your optimal life. The reality is, it is a learning process and new lessons will always unfold.

By developing your personal strategy for success, you take action towards living your best life by declaring that it's not enough to simply get by or survive the chaos. That instead, you want to live a remarkable life filled with joy, balance, whole-heartedness, clarity, freedom, gratitude, good health, security, connectedness, purpose, intention, vulnerability, compassion, authenticity, courage, mindfulness and calm, leaving you free to truly engage in your daily life and enjoy what really matters.

The second purpose of this book is to remind you not to be a passenger in life! Jump into the driver's seat and live each day with intention, clarity and purpose, so you can truly engage and enjoy every success.

With intentional enthusiasm,
Shannah Kennedy

THANK YOU

—

I'd like to thank all the people who have helped me get to this place:

Julie Gibbs, for giving me the chance to publish after having such a great experience at self-publishing. You are an inspiration, Julie; thank you for believing in me. To the Penguin team, especially Evi O, Katrina O'Brien, Jocelyn Hungerford and Anna Scobie for really understanding that I wanted to create a self-help book like no other. The photo shoot team: Sharyn Cairns, Stephanie Stamatis, Ella Bendrups and Caitlin Mills, for a fun time and totally amazing results.

My family, of course, who always encourage me to be bigger and better and grow way beyond my comfort zone. To Mum, Dad, Carol, Michael and my extended family Cathie, Aaron, Romy and Tim, for always encouraging me and being right behind me – it means the world.

Thank you to Michelle for letting me write this book in her holiday home (I just can't write at home), and to my girlfriends who are always supportive: Carolyn, Deb, Lyndall, Chris and so many more who believe in me, listen to me and are there for me no matter what is happening. You are all a part of my dream team in life and I hope I offer you the same level of comfort you all offer me.

Most importantly, thank you to my clients and social media followers. You are the reason I keep going, growing and pushing myself to new levels. Those of you I work with personally are gold in my life – you share your innermost thoughts, challenges and wins with me, and this is incredibly rewarding and something I never take for granted. I hope this book gives all of you an incredibly solid foundation for your life.

Index

LANTERN

UK | USA | Canada | Ireland | Australia
India | New Zealand | South Africa | China

Penguin Books is part of the Penguin
Random House group of companies
whose addresses can be found at global.
penguinrandomhouse.com.

Penguin
Random House
Australia

First published by Penguin Group
(Australia), 2015

Design by Evi O. @ Penguin Group (Australia)
Photography by Sharyn Cairns, except
for family photographs pages 186-9
by Shannah Kennedy and family
Styling by Stephanie Stamatis
Typeset in Harriet by Evi O.
Colour separation by Splitting Image Colour
Studio, Clayton, Victoria

Printed and bound in China by RR Donelley
Asia Printing Solutions Limited

National Library of Australia
Cataloguing-in-Publication entry

Kennedy, Shannah, author.
The life plan / Shannah Kennedy ;
Sharyn Cairns.
9780670078301 (paperback)
Includes index.
Self-actualisation (Psychology).
Life skills.
Conduct of life.
Self-realisation.
Other creators/contributors:
Cairns, Sharyn, photographer.

158.1

penguin.com.au/lantern

We would like to thank the following for kindly
supplying props for photography: Wootten,
Beth-Emily, Arro Home, Phillip Van Huynh.

The author would like to thank the following for their
kind permission to reproduce from their works:
Cheryl Richardson, *The Art of Extreme Self-Care*,
copyright July 2012, Hay House, Inc., Carlsbad, CA;
Margie Warrell; and Dr Carmen Harra.

Where others have been quoted, every effort has been
made to contact them, and full acknowledgement of
their work has been given in the text.